MILE HIGH

"I wasn't born with hate in me. I had to learn it. I learned it because I got tired of just taking things people dished out, taking, taking..."

"I haven't been afraid of very many things in my life. I've been afraid of being lonely. That happens to me a lot. Even now. I tell my wife, and she puts me in her arms and tells me it will never happen. Believe me, meeting that woman is the best thing that ever happened to me..."

"One thing I've learned, I don't forget the people I've met on the way up 'cause I know when I'm down and I can't play anymore I'm gonna pass those same people. They may look at me differently, but I won't forget them. And I don't forget people who've been true friends to me..."

Lyle Alzado—the man, the athlete, the tough street kid—speaks out in a moving, spirited portrait of a player—and a team—who wouldn't settle for less than everything.

MILE HIGH—*The Story of Lyle Alzado and the Amazing Denver Broncos.*

MILE HIGH:
The Story of Lyle Alzado and the Amazing Denver Broncos

**Lyle Alzado
with
Paul Zimmerman**

A BERKLEY BOOK
published by
BERKLEY PUBLISHING CORPORATION

Copyright © 1978, by Lyle Alzado and Paul Zimmerman

All rights reserved

Published by arrangement with the authors' agent

All rights reserved which includes the right
to reproduce this book or portions thereof in
any form whatsoever. For information address

Berkley Publishing Corporation
200 Madison Avenue
New York, New York 10016

SBN 425-03920-X

BERKLEY MEDALLION BOOKS are published by
Berkley Publishing Corporation
200 Madison Avenue
New York, N. Y. 10016

BERKLEY MEDALLION BOOK ® TM 757,375

Printed in the United States of America

Berkley Edition, January, 1978

Thanks to the four horsemen—LS, RR, CF, PT—for unstinting loyalty and service above and beyond the call of duty.

Table of Contents

PROLOGUE	1
ONE: Saturday Night Special	9
TWO: Lawrence High: Roughneck on the Gridiron	27
THREE: The Fighting Greyhounds of Yankton	57
FOUR: A Scout's Diary	73
FIVE: Making It	79
SIX: A Girl from Yankton	87
SEVEN: Tombstone	99
EIGHT: The NFL Way	107
NINE: Lyle Alzado: A Coach's View	115
TEN: Always the Knee	123
ELEVEN: The Dirty Dozen	131
TWELVE: A Tough Business	141
THIRTEEN: What Next?	159
FOURTEEN: Broncomania	175
FIFTEEN: One Week to Kickoff	183
SIXTEEN: Super Bowl XII	209
EPILOGUE I	225
EPILOGUE II	229

MILE HIGH:
The Story of Lyle Alzado
and the Amazing Denver Broncos

Prologue

Lyle Alzado jogged slowly down the ramp, out onto the Superdome Astroturf. Super Bowl XII was an hour away. He didn't look at the stands, although a group of Bronco fans started shouting his name as soon as they spotted him.

The night before, he had begun his pregame psyching up by closing out the world. "I don't even want to talk to him the night before a game," his wife says. That morning he had watched an old Tarzan movie on television, and on the bus ride to the stadium he had stared out the window—talking to nobody, being approached by nobody. That is his mood. After seven years, the people around him know enough to leave him alone.

He jogged onto the Superdome's artificial turf and immediately headed for his place in Red Miller's calisthenics formation. Fourth row, fourth in from the left, Tommy Jackson to the left, Billy Thompson to the right. It never varies.

Work hard now, then slack off as the game gets closer. Biggest game, Alzado is thinking. Never play in a bigger one...

NEW ORLEANS had always been an uncomfortable Super Bowl town. It froze over for Super Bowl IV, Chiefs *vs.* Vikings. The fountain at the Chiefs' headquarters—the Fountainbleu Hotel—was a chunk of ice. Kansas City coach Hank Stram held his first press conference in a dining-room suite off the main lobby, and the Chiefs—always a stylish club—served the writers Eggs Benedict. But the heating unit broke down, and the lingering memory is of a hundred newsmen, shivering in overcoats and hats and trying to fight their way through ice-cold Eggs Benedict.

At the game itself, Pat O'Brien failed to keep up with the music when he recited the National Anthem; and the halftime show—a re-creation of the Battle of New Orleans—almost resulted in tragedy when the giant hot-air balloons failed to rise and went careening into the stands.

It drizzled before the game, and scalpers who were charging up to $75 a ticket a week earlier had to eat their tickets by kickoff. Walking through the mud around Tulane Stadium you saw them standing there in the rain, hawking 40-yard-line seats for $2 apiece—or whatever you wanted to pay.

Pickpockets ran wild in Tulane Stadium next time New Orleans hosted the Super Bowl. January 1975, Steelers *vs.* Vikings; half-a-dozen writers and countless fans had their wallets lifted. Most of the wallets were recovered—minus the cash, naturally. Tulane Stadium Security was beautifully equipped to handle the emergency.

"Oh, this is nothing new," a woman in the security office said. "We've had as many as three thousand wallets stolen during a game. New Orleans is the pickpocket capital of the world."

Back came Super Bowl XII to a New Orleans choked with traffic from its never-ending run of winter conventions, as early Mardi Gras season, and the King Tut exhibit at the New Orleans Museum of Art. Nine days before the Super Bowl, Gerald Ford had spoken at the Rivergate. "I'm healthy and I'm going to be around," he'd told 3,000 real estate agents, "especially in 1980." Two days later, the Boy Scouts of America opened up shop next to the Super Bowl press headquarters in the Hyatt Regency. International Transactional Analysis, Woodfold Chemical, World on Wheels, Vita Craft, Whirlpool, Philip Morris—these and many, many others all dumped their delegates and delegates' wives on an already teeming Super Bowl city.

The King Tut exhibit had attracted 700,000 people to the Museum of Art during the four months it had been in town. The Fairmont Hotel ran the concession tent in the museum and pocketed nearly $200,000 clear profit. Mardi Gras—which usually starts in late February or early March—was to begin on February 7 this year. With the Super Bowl still eight days away, early Mardi Gras revelers began arriving for the Bards of Bohemia midnight dinner-dance which would officially open the Carnival Season.

Into New Orleans they poured, choking the hotels, the restaurants, and the streets—and the city became a sea of orange as New Orleans accepted the Bronco fans and vice versa. Cowboy fans seemed subdued in the wake of all this Orange Crush. On Saturday, in the big court of the Royal Sonesta, Broncomania had taken over: a Bronco fan paraded around in a big hat with a revolving police light on top, and everywhere Bronco rooters were raising hell, carrying on.

Snapshot: as four gigantic Texans in blue-and-white Cowboy shirts stand up. "Should we do it?" one asks, and the rest nod. "Okay. Uh-one, uh-two..." And their voices rise to a roar:

Prologue

"We're not ugly, we're not mean.
We'll say somethin' for the other team...
Broncos, Broncos...BAHT MAH AH-YUSS!"

Pretty girl in a Bronco tee-shirt stands up. "FUUUCCCKKK YOU!" she yells.

"What's that?" one of the Texans asks.

"FUUUCCCKKK YOU!" she yells again, twice as loud.

A mile away, at the Hyatt Regency, the sporting press—which included representatives from as far away as Mexico and Japan—ground out hundreds of advance stories. A huge meeting room was outfitted with tables and typewriters and officially designated the press workroom. From this room the Super Bowl was advanced, almost nonstop, round the clock, every angle on every player worked and reworked, then worked again.

Most newsmen preferred to arrive later in the week, write an advance or two, cover the game, and then go home. But the game must be publicized: the National Football League has a huge television guarantee to cover, and two weeks of advance publicity is its way of paying back the network and sponsors. Thus fresh angles are cherished, curios are in great demand, and—though none has surfaced so far—a player with two heads would be terrific. Any player with something unusual to say is pounced upon.

At Super Bowl XII, a hundred typewriters pounded out the story of Craig Morton's resurgence as a living, breathing Bronco quarterback after years in the doldrums with Dallas and the New York Giants; analyzed and re-analyzed his sore hip, pulled thigh muscle, and low interception rate; scrutinized his income-tax problems and renewed faith-in-life as a Born-Again Christian ("He's probably having less fun now," said ex-Dallas teammate Cliff Harris, All-Pro free safetyman, "but he's getting more sleep").

Bronco defensive end Lyle Alzado, with his hair-raising tales of life on the streets of New York, was widely quoted. So was Harris, a vicious hitter once called "a rolling ball of butcher knives" by Texas coach Darrell Royal. "Craig Morton will not finish the Super Bowl," was Harris's showpiece quote—the same statement he made last time he played in the Super Bowl, only last time he'd named Steeler quarterback Terry Bradshaw (and the prediction came true, though it was a blitzing D. D. Lewis, and not Harris, who removed Bradshaw from Super Bowl X).

Denver's left guard Tom Glassic—a serious-faced second-year pro from the University of Virginia—was found to be a military buff who viewed each game as the re-creation of some famous battle from history and even assigned each participant a battle station. Dallas coach Tom Landry became Napoleon ("fantastic attention to minute detail, but on a grand scale..."); Denver coach Red Miller stood in for Sir John Moore, whose crack rifle brigades—painstakingly and lovingly created, allowing the utmost in individuality—defeated Napoleon in the Peninsula Campaign; linemen constituted the infantry; the linebackers and running backs, heavy cavalry; quarterbacks became generals. For Tom Glassic, Denver *vs.* Kansas City was Borodino ("a slugfest... tremendous massed action without a clear-cut victory..."); Denver *vs.* Baltimore was Austerlitz ("lulled 'em to sleep and then struck..."); Denver *vs.* Oakland, for the AFC title, best resembled Waterloo ("Napoleon could have won it if he had two more hours, just as Oakland could have won it if they'd gotten the ball back"). Super Bowl against Dallas? Possibly Balaklava: "I see it ending in a massed cavalry charge, the most glorious thing in battle," said Glassic.

John Jeansonne, an enterprising young writer for *Newsday*, the Long Island paper, examined the psychology of color—of orange—and concluded that people who have been deprived for extended periods favor bright, gaudy colors. The Bronco fans had been deprived for seventeen years.

In the press lounge off the main workroom, four hours before kickoff, Abe Gibron held court. Abe coaches the defensive linemen for Tampa Bay, coaches them as he used to play the game: mean, rough, unforgiving. Defensive line has not been one of Tampa Bay's problems.

"Who do you like, Abie?" someone asked him.

Abe snorted. His conversation is a collection of snorts and grunts: that's when he likes you. When he doesn't, he turns his back on you and you're left looking at 350 pounds of turned back—a most effective means of getting the message across. But this time Abie snorted, because he likes to talk about the Broncos. They're his kind of team. He favors roughnecks.

"Alzado," he says. "I like the Alzado kid. They turn him loose, he can bust up that Dallas offense pretty good."

"One man doesn't make a difference," replied another writer. "One man can't do anything to an offense."

"Kiss my ass," said Abie.

"How about the Dallas Flex Defense?" someone went on. "The coordinated defense, revolving around the Flex?"

"Lemme tell you something," Abie said. "If all of a sudden a coach came up with the idea of all the defensive linemen showing up with their flies open and *won* with that defense, next year all the other teams would have *their* defensive linemen on the field with unzipped flies." He thought for a minute. "The Flex don't mean a damn unless you got people to play it. What do they have... Two All-Pros in that defensive line, the third guy was the number-one pick in the whole draft in his year, and the fourth guy—Pugh—

has been playing in the NFL for a hundred and fifty years. When they need a pass-rush they take him out and rest him up. That's what makes a defense: *people*. And that Alzado kid on Denver is my kind of people. He don't take no crap from nobody."

ONE:

Saturday Night Special

I wasn't born with hate in me. I had to learn it. I learned it because I got tired of just taking things people dished out, taking, taking....
—Lyle

LYLE ALZADO is the right defensive end of the Denver Broncos. He is 6-3 and carries a program weight of 260 pounds, but the day before the Super Bowl he weighed 248. He predicted he'd come in light—to match the speed of the Cowboys' attack, the quickness of Ralph Neely, the 6-6 offensive tackle he'll be playing against.

Alzado's career has been filled with ironies. In 1974 and '75—in his fourth and fifth year as a starter at right defensive end—he led the team in quarterback sacks and harassments, playing at "All-Pro quality," as the Broncos' press guide noted. But in 1976 he was switched inside, to middle guard in the new three-man defensive alignment, and he tore two ligaments in his knee on the first play of the season. He was 27. Some people suggested his career was over.

He came back to right defensive end in 1977, burdened by a postoperative knee and the knowledge that every defensive lineman in the 3-4 can count on a heavy share of double-teaming each afternoon. Very few 3-4 linemen are picked All-Pro, an honor that had eluded Alzado throughout his career.

"The pass-rushers make All-Pro," he said before the '77 season. "The eye-catchers. And on the 3-4 you're not worth a damn unless you can play the run, unless you can tie up the guys in front of you and let your linebackers roam free. When I first came up, all I wanted to do was get to the passer. But now I pride myself on the way I can play the run. You have to sacrifice in this game, you know? Okay, I've sacrificed a shot at All-Pro for the sake of our defense. I don't think I'll ever make it."

But he did make it—in his seventh year. He was a consensus choice for the combined NFC-AFC team. The Broncos were 12-2, and their defense was the best at stopping the run in the 28-team NFL. Five Broncos were picked by the NFL players and coaches to go to the Pro Bowl to represent the AFC against the NFC. All were on defense: Alzado, linebackers Randy Gradishar and Tommy Jackson, cornerback Louie Wright, and strong safety Bill Thompson. For Alzado it was both a surprise and a triumph, a victory that could be complete with a Super Bowl ring.

Twenty-eight years ago, Lyle Martin Alzado was born in Brooklyn, the second of five children. His mother, Martha Sokolow, is Jewish, his father, Maurice Alzado, Italian-Spanish. Alzado is a Spanish name. "I've never been able to find another Alzado," Lyle says. "When we go on trips my wife and I look through the phone directories for another Alzado, but we've never found one. Alvado, Alvarado ... but never an Alzado."

He lived the first ten years of his life on Herzl Street in the Brownsville section of Brooklyn. It was an area culturally rich but economically deprived. Herzl Street—named after Theodor Herzl, who founded the Zionist movement in the 1890s—is near the now-extinct public baths that served as a meeting place during the first third of the 20th century. Right around the corner was the old Brownsville Labor Lyceum, where Sol Hurok started his career—as its manager—and where Indian poet Rabindranath Tagore once spoke before a packed house.

Sociologically and geographically removed from the fiercely Hasidic neighborhoods of Williamsburg and Borough Park, Brownsville was once a haven for liberal and radical Jews; it was a Jewish cultural island.

And it was a neighborhood of decaying tenements. Cross the Van Sinderen Avenue elevated line and you're in East New York, with its neat one- and two-family houses. But Brownsville always was, and is, poor. Now it is mostly black.

When Alzado was ten, the family moved to Cedarhurst on Long Island's South Shore—right across the Queens border from the Gilded Ghetto, as it was called—then to Woodmere, one of the five towns that make up Inwood (Lawrence, Inwood, Woodmere, and Hewlett). It was known as the Classic Jewish Migration.

Alzado's life began in the streets. It began with violence and hatred.

"You learn to hate by watching your father come home drunk and start punching your mother around. I saw him rip a damn electric heater out of the wall when there were five kids lying in the house there freezing.

"You want to know a significant event in my life? The first guy I ever punched. His name was Massoni ...get it right...M-A-S-S-O-N-I. How old was I? Ten maybe. That's when we lived in Brooklyn, on Herzl Street. It's a hell of a thing to remember, isn't it, a hell of a way to start off the story of your life? Remembering hate. Remembering violence. But these things are so clear. It's the good things that are hazy.

"I'll tell you the very first thing I remember. I remember sitting next to a fence... You know how the houses are built in Brooklyn? The building is here, and then the steps come down, and there's a fence.

"Well, I must have been seven or eight. I can remember leaning up on the fence one afternoon by myself, and the fence was about rotted away and I was kind of digging around in there with my hands. I remember finding a switchblade. That's the first thing I remember, finding a switchblade dug into the fence. And I took the switchblade out and tried to open it. It wouldn't open, it was rusted up, so I pried the thing open. I used to play with it, we used to carve sticks with it and stuff, you know, just keep it in my pocket. First thing I remember."

There were five Alzado children. Peter is the oldest, 30, a former track athlete for Queens College and Kansas, 6-0, 165 pounds. "Used to be a hell of a runner," Lyle Alzado says. "Ran a 46-flat quarter mile, competed in the Maccabiah Games. He's trying to make it as an actor now—Off-Broadway stuff."

Next came Lyle, born Lyle Martin Alzado ("Don't ask me how I got the name Lyle. I guess my father just liked it"). Then Billy, 25, who now works as an electrical engineer for the government in New Jersey. ("Probably the best all-around athlete in the family. Decathlon. What a gifted athlete. I mean the guy was brilliant: 6-2, 190 pounds. He could do everything. He was coming home one night and he cracked up his motorcycle. Spent seven weeks in a coma. When he came out of it he'd lost everything, athletically.")

Janice is 24, a cocktail waitress in Denver. Unmarried. ("Likes to play around too much for that. You have to keep an eye on her.") Finally Sandy, 18 and just out of high school, trying to become a model. Lives with her mother in Long Branch, New Jersey.

The five of them grew up in Brooklyn and Long Island with a mother who worked ten hours a day for $80 a week in a flower shop and a father who'd show up when he felt like it. "Half-drunk and crazy when he did come around," Alzado says. "Always flashed a big roll, though we never got any of it and never knew where it came from.

"The only real family we had was on my mother's side. Jewish. We were raised Jewish. My mother's name was Martha Sokolow; her parents were born in Russia, Sol and Anna Sokolow.

"My grandpa was a hatmaker. I can remember one time we were sitting at the dinner table in their house. My grandma used to wear those hats with the pin in it, and she had one on the table for some reason. My grandpa told her, 'Take it off the table. I'll make you another one.' Funny, the things you remember. I remember the clothes they wore; old, patched up sometimes, but always very neat, very clean.

"And I remember the smells of food in that house. God, those smells! Stuffed cabbage, that's a smell that you never forget. The onions, cooked onions, fried onions, garlic and stuffed cabbage. Bagels—ah, bagels!—she used to make these. And the chopped liver...She used to make chopped liver for me, then put it in the refrigerator with a little cellophane over it and I used to take it out and just eat the whole thing at once.

"I can remember my grandparents moving from Brooklyn out to Queens, and I can remember my brother Billy and I went down and we were playing under the steps where you cross the bridge. It was before they built the highway, and it was all woods there, all weeds and stuff like that.

"My brother and I were camping out near the woods there, just there for the afternoon. We were fooling around for a couple of hours, and we started lighting these matches and we caught bushes and stuff on fire. It all went up in flames, and my brother and I ran.

"The fire department came. They saw us run, and I can remember us running up into the apartment building and looking down and watching the firemen point at the building, saying, 'They went in there.' They never came into the apartment. They must have been scared to. I mean, it wasn't a massive fire, but it was a fire, you know?

"I must have been 12 or so. I ran upstairs crying. My mother said, 'What's the matter?' I wouldn't tell her. And when the fire engines came I just went and hid.

"I saw my grandparents a lot when I was little because my mom would always go there when my dad was acting crazy. I remember when I had nothing to eat, nothing to wear, my grandparents would give me a winter jacket, buy me pants, buy me shoes. My grandparents were very, very good people.

"One night—I must have been 13 or 14 because we'd already moved from Booklyn to Springfield Gardens in Queens, and then to Cedarhurst, Long Island—we had this old electric burner, you flip a switch and it comes on. My dad came home one night crazy, punching holes in the walls, crap like that, trying to beat up on my mom, on us.

"He worked himself into a rage and pulled the heater right out of the wall. Just ripped it apart. About 11 or 12 o'clock at night. Freezing in the house. Why did he do it? I don't know why. How can you understand a man who wants to be good but can't, who doesn't know how, who's just filled with rage all the time? How do you explain it? I can't.

"His name was Maurice Alzado, pronounced Al-zah-do, but everyone here in Denver pronounces it Al-zay-do, so I just let it slide. People called him Pat. His ancestors were Spaniards who settled in Italy. I've seen stories that said I was part Puerto Rican as well. Fine—the more nationalities the better—but it isn't accurate. I guess some people figure the only Spaniards in New York are Puerto Rican.

"Anyway, my dad was about 6-1, 210 pounds. A boxer, although he never would tell me where or when. One of the few things he ever did for me was bring home a pair of gloves when I was about eight. 'Okay,' he said, 'now you're going to learn to fight,' and he laced them on and started popping me. At the time I hated it, but he did me a real favor, boy.

"What an athlete that guy could have been. Tremendously fast on his feet. He could run like hell. Massive through the arms and shoulders. His arms looked like they had grapefruits in them. And what a hitter, what a slugger he was.

"Who knows what kind of work he did? Probably spent half the time in some kind of racket. One day you'd see him lugging car engines around, the next day he'd be doing odd jobs. Once he told me he had a paint company, but I knew that was bullshit. For a while he ran a bar in the Inwood section in Long Island. Fight-a-night kind of place. You'd always see some kind of action there. Half the time he was in it.

"Sometimes he'd have people working for him on these odd jobs, and one time he hired a few guys to help him out. Who knows what they really were? Rackets guys, probably.

"I remember four guys came to the door one night looking for him, and I said, 'Dad, some guys are here to see you.' We had this big picture window in our kitchen, and these guys came in the kitchen—right next to the picture window—and my dad came in the room and said, 'What's wrong?' They said, 'We want more money, you know, we deserve more money out of this job.' My dad said, 'You ain't getting shit. You got paid what I told you you were going to get paid and that's it.'

"They were pretty big, these four guys, and they went at my dad. I'm telling you something, my dad put these guys through the door, through the window, on the floor, up in the air. Then he called an ambulance and left the house; he said come get these four guys... badly hurt people... come get them. The police stayed at my house more than they stayed at the station, I think. I mean, he was devastating.

"The only time I can ever remember my dad wanting to do something to help me in school, I had flunked a math test. When I came home, I was doing my math homework, and I didn't understand something and I asked him to help me. My dad was pretty good at math, but the way he would help me was he would yell and scream and pound and hit me until I got the problem right. And if my mother tried to stop him, he'd hit her, too.

"I knew after a while I had to start protecting my mom, because my dad would beat her unmercifully sometimes. I remember my dad came home all drunk one day, and he just took my mom by the throat and started banging her head on the door. At the time I didn't know what to do because I was so afraid of him. He was so powerful.

"She moved us into an apartment in Woodmere for

a while so that she could keep him away from her—from us, too. Dumpy old apartment. I would see the roaches when I'd come home at night from football practice; sometimes I'd see the roaches on a loaf of bread I had to eat the next morning.

"But my dad followed my mom home one night when we lived there. I was lying in bed, and my sister came in and said, 'Lyle, Lyle, Mommy's coming home and Daddy's parked across the street. You've got to come quick.' I said, 'What do you want me to do?' I never really had to fight with him before. She said, 'You've got to help her, you've got to help her. I can see him down the block.'

"He got out of the car and started running down the block, and my mom started running for the door of the apartment building. So I ran downstairs, and just as I got to the corner he grabbed her. I stepped in front and he swung and hit me in the face. But I fought, I fought that night. I lost the decision, but I did pretty well. And the police came and arrested him. He had me thrown in jail for assault and battery. He was there, too, but he had me thrown in for that. I was crying and everything.

"I was a little bigger then, about 190, and it must have sunk in a little bit that I was dangerous to mess with. He stayed away a little bit after that, you know, although he did come around a couple more times. I keep talking about how bad my dad was, but he really wanted to be good. He just didn't know how. He just didn't.

"My mom wouldn't let me know my father's family, but you know what I remember about my dad's family? We had this beautiful dog, a boxer, I mean this dog was fabulous, one of the finest dogs I've ever been around, and I've had dogs my whole life. This dog was always with us; he helped us, you know, brought the newspaper in and all that kind of stuff. My dad gave the dog to his mom and the dog died. A year later, the dog was dead. Don't ask me why, because I don't know.

"My dad's mom was a very big woman—born in Italy, real old-country—and she would always sit in this one chair in her dark apartment in Brooklyn. She would sit in this big chair, and my dad would always make us sit on her lap. And sometimes she would give us $10. I'd sit on her lap for $10.

"He was different around her, changed almost, quiet—but hard, always hard, always tough. He'd try to act right, but he just didn't know how. He had a younger brother, too. Frank. Just like my dad. Unbelievable how similar they were. That's it. That's all I ever knew about my dad's family.

"The two families were always apart. My dad would never go with us to my mother's parents' house. He would never let me get bar-mitzvahed. I don't think he had anything against Jews—I mean, he wasn't a devout Catholic who went to church all the time—he just said no to the bar mitzvah and that was it. I don't know if he was religious or nonreligious. He never let me get that close to him.

"Religion was very important to my mother. For a while, me and my brother Billy would go to temple with her, to Temple Sinai in Cedarhurst. You know what finished me there? I was caught robbing coat pockets during the service.

"They'd hang their coats downstairs, and I'd leave—like I was going to the bathroom—and go downstairs, go through the pockets and steal anything I could find. I did it for months before I was caught. Some guy just came down there one time and nailed me. Unbelievable, isn't it?

"Religion didn't mean a damn thing to me. I'd go to the temple just to make my mother happy—and for the coat-pocket money, of course. We'd have these big seders at my grandparents' house. I liked the food, but you could have the rest of it. Once they tried to get me to stand up and ask the Four Questions. I couldn't do it. I was always afraid to get up in front of people.

"And I never understood any of those things, and

anyway I didn't like it because I'm not a religious person. I believe in God, but that's where it ends, right there.

"I've tried to go to temple, and I search for a meaning behind religion, but I can never find it. It's so contradictory. Everybody I talk to, places I go to—even with the team I go to these functions, chapel before the game—it's just not there. It frustrates me and bothers me because I can't see what they do.

"There is more to it. God's more than that, or at least I think He is. It's funny, but I never believed in God until I went to college. I never believed in anything, nothing. But no, I never liked it. I enjoyed the food at the seders, and I liked my uncles; I liked them a lot and I loved my grandparents. But you know what I loved best? I loved going out on jobs with my dad, dumping engines out of cars in dump lots and stuff like that. I went with him whenever he'd let me.

"When I was young my concentration span was about this big, about a sixteenth of an inch. I just never had any. I just didn't care. I used to daydream about going out there and boxing, fighting. I used to think about that all the time. It was a waste of my time, to go to school or temple or anything like that. I was so frustrated in that classroom, and it was so boring to me. I can remember just wishing I could get out of there somehow, just jump out the window. Except for maybe a couple of my grade-school teachers, a couple of teachers in college, and one or two in high school—otherwise every teacher I ever had always yelled at me.

"Once when I was in grade school I had this teacher, and I went out on the playground and I was playing around and I had a pair of pants that I split all the way up to here. I went home and changed and put on these pants I wore for four or five days in a row before that—filthy dirty, smelled and everything, but I had nothing else. I had to wear them. I was one of the last kids back into the classroom, and the teacher looked down at me and said, 'You look like a pig. Why don't you ever change your clothes?' I looked around at the other kids in the classroom and I didn't know what to do. She told me to sit down. They were all laughing and giggling at me; kids laughed at me all the time because I had nothing.

"And that's when I started fighting, when people laughed at me, because I just got so tired of it. I started beating on people; they were afraid of me, so they wouldn't laugh at me. I wasn't bigger than other kids, but I was stronger. My dad was such a naturally powerful person, such a strong person, and I got that from him. I had that same kind of strength in me. I could get in street fights and beat up four or five guys at a time. I mean I'd get hit and I'd just go berserk. It was ridiculous.

"I remember one day I went to the playground, and I had been sick—must have had a stomach virus—but I went to school, you know, I liked going to school. I hardly ever missed school, not in high school, not in college, not anywhere. I liked going. Don't ask me why. Maybe it was the idea that that was the only place anybody cared at all what happened to me. Even though I was a lousy student, with lousy concentration and all, they seemed to care. Just the idea that someone was trying to do something for me, to teach me something, kept me going back. Besides, what the hell else was there? The streets? My father?

"Anyway, this one day when I went to the playground in school, I was sitting down because I felt so sick. I was sitting against the wall, watching the other kids play. The kids came over saying, 'You smell, you smell,' that kind of thing, laughing at me and laughing at me and laughing at me. I went home, but it stayed in my mind—the girls, the girls laughing at me as much as any of them.

"And then one day, I don't know what happened to me. I just woke up and said that's it, fuck these people.

And I just started fighting. The first guy was this kid Massoni.

"He made fun of a shirt I was wearing. It was torn in the back. So I walked over to him, looked at him, and remembered everything I'd been thinking for days before that. I just went nuts. I don't know what happened; I just started punching this guy and kicking him and punching him and punching, banging his head off the sidewalk, you know, screaming, 'Leave me alone, don't you ever...' A teacher—Mr. Davis, one of the people I really liked in school, one of the few teachers who really took time with me—pulled me off him.

"The kid was unconscious. And every time it happened after that I just kept fighting and fighting, until the teachers were afraid. The teachers told my mom, you should bring him somewhere and have him taken care of. Psychiatric help. I went to a psychiatrist, but you know what it was—a school-type psychiatrist. I used to go to his office, and he would put me in this room and make me play with blocks, and then he'd show me things. I don't remember what the things were, but he'd say, 'What does this mean to you?' And he asked me to write it down. I never knew how to spell very well, but I'd try to write it out. Then he'd start again, 'Now what does this mean to you?'

"I went to him for about a year or two, once or twice a week. It didn't help, it got worse. I'd go out and fight, I'd sneak out at night to fight. I was just wild.

"One night when I was in high school, Ira Gordon went to a party. Ira was one of my best friends in those days. Still is. Five of us used to hang out together—me and Ira and Larry Schepps and Mark Lyons and Richie Mollo. The Immortal Five. We all went to high school together, all played sports. I became close with Sal Ciampi, too; he'd played at Lawrence and then Purdue, and then come back to coach at Lawrence. But that was later.

Anyway, that night Ira went to this party. I was at a party down the block—I liked this little chick down there so I went to check her out, you know. The other four guys left and said, we're going to another party, and I said I'll see you guys later. I had my little black beret on, and I thought I was cool and all. So they went to this other party, got kicked out, and came back about an hour later. They said, 'Hey, Lyle, these people kicked us out of this party, man, and there's a lot of women there.' So I said, 'Well, nothing's happening here, I'll go down with you, and we'll see what's happening.' So I went to the other party. I don't know, the people at this other party were a little older than me—18 or 19, something like that—I was about 16 or 17. They said, 'Get out!' At that time in my life, when people told me what to do, jumped in my face like that, I would just blow up. I just got tired of people telling me what to do. And five or six guys came at me. I tell you the truth, I put these guys everywhere, *everywhere*—on the floor, on top of tables, in the swimming pool they had, everywhere.

"And you know what I did? I took the basket of chicken that they had out for the people and said, 'Thanks for the chicken,' and walked out. Ira Gordon and George Mayweather and Larry Schepps—those are the three guys that were there with me.

"Another time I was at a firehouse dance. It was when I was in high school, and I went out with this girl Jane. Ira was with me. I was dancing, you know, and some guy bumped into her. I really dug her, too, and some guy bumped into her. So I let this guy have it, put him on the floor. The whole place broke up, total disaster. Unbelievable.

"I'll never forget the night I got stabbed, the first time I ever got stabbed. I was in a bar; I must have been 16—I always looked older than I was—and I got into this bar which I wasn't supposed to be in, in Far Rockaway. I was sitting in the back listening to some music and watching the kids dance. I was checking things out, having a beer, and I was looking at this girl—beautiful blonde—and her boyfriend looked over real quick and saw me looking at her. She kind of smiled back, you know, she must have been 19 or 20. Her boyfriend went into the men's room and then came back out, and on the way he stopped and said, 'Keep looking and I'm going to break your face.' So I stood up and said something smart, like I'm going to rearrange your face or something clever like that.

"So this guy reached in his pocket, pulled out a little knife, and put it in me, just put it in me. And at the moment I didn't feel it. When you get stabbed you don't feel it until you pull it out. I took the bottle I had in front of me and just broke it across his face, then ran out of the bar.

"The knife went in me about an inch. I've got five or six knife scars on me: one on my leg that you can still see, plus a couple more. I said that's it, I learned my lesson, at 16—that's a long time ago, right? I started carrying a straight razor. It was a metal piece about this long, about three inches, and it was square. All you had to do was just press a button and the blade would come up in an angle. You just flicked it.

"I was stabbed four times. Another time was when I was on the Rockaway boardwalk playing the penny arcades with about 10 or 12 guys I thought were my friends, and I looked around and they were gone. I just figured they were on the beach playing around, but they weren't, you know. They were just gone.

"I looked on the boardwalk and couldn't find them, so I went back out to the parking lot. The car we drove down in was gone. So I said, 'Well, I better get out of here.'

"I was gonna walk down the boardwalk out of Far Rock, going into Atlantic Beach, but I was stopped by three or four Puerto Ricans standing on the side. There was a girl standing there. I was carrying my little straight razor.

"One guy said, 'Hey, Whitey, come here man, come here,' and then they started calling me names, trying to get me to make the first move. The girl came over with a broken Coke bottle and put it to my neck. She said, 'Don't move.' You know what happens when they have you set up like that? They start cutting you. I said to myself, I gotta go for broke. So I threw my hands up, knocked the bottle out of her hand, and pushed her over the side of the boardwalk. This was a 10- or 15-foot drop, and it knocked her onto the beach.

"Those guys came at me, and I got in the middle of the boardwalk. You know how big the boardwalk is—25 feet wide, maybe. I got in the middle, took my straight razor out, and when I started swinging it in a circle they gathered around me.

"I got cut three times on my hands, and you can still see the scars. I have one on my leg, and I got stabbed in the side. It wasn't a deep one, just a slice. After they cut me in the side I went down on my knees; when you get sliced you feel that; whereas a stab wound you don't feel until much later.

"So I went down on my knees, and I took the straight razor and cut a couple of them in the legs. Just then this friend of mine showed up, an enormous guy, John Wilson—Big John Wilson they called him. He's about 6-8, 350 pounds, held the National Freshman shot-put record at 65 feet. Anyway, he came in there and pulled me out and chased them away from there.

"Another time I got stabbed outside a bar in Inwood. I guess I was 16. As a matter of fact, it was the Golden Dream, a bar my daddy used to own. A bar where all the riffraff hung out.

"I went out in back to get some fresh air, into this kind of alley—more like a driveway, really. And this kid I went to junior high school with, big strong kid named Michael Woodby, followed me out there and turned me around and cut me on top of the shoulders. He just cut me. No reason. He was drunked up, just went crazy.

"I picked up a board and hit him over the head and knocked him out. It was a bad cut. That knife was this long. If he'd cut me two inches farther up, or if he'd hit me in the neck...

"We didn't go in for guns much in our neighborhood; but I was in a fight once in a place called the Haven, and a good friend of mine, Chris Kipernides, threw a guy through a window. Chris Kipernides was one of the toughest kids I ever met in my life. Boy was he tough, I mean a vicious fighter. Anyway, we ran out of the bar, and a guy came out of there with a pellet gun and shot Chris in the back three or four times. He didn't kill him but...

"I remember once at a place in Hempstead—and this is scary, this is as close as I got to anything with actual or real heavy artillery—a gang from Hempstead came out to Inwood. They got into a fight with five or six guys from Inwood and beat them up, and a couple of guys I hung around with were so mad they got into this car and went to Hempstead High School during lunch hour and took a sawed-off shotgun and blew out the windows in the classroom. Kaboom! Kaboom!

TWO:

Lawrence High: Roughneck on the Gridiron

In high school I was still a violent guy, but it was channeled now. I'll tell you something I think changed my life: I got into a fight and was thrown in jail overnight for disturbing the peace. I was a wise-ass, and I got thrown into jail. If you've never been in the jails in Nassau County, don't ever go. You won't like it. They're square cubicles, and there's a camera that rotates back and forth to see you—they have pictures up front at the desk.

I was going to be a smart-ass, so I took off all my clothes and started doing jumping jacks and push-ups and sit-ups and stuff, jumping up and down. There's a wooden bench that you sleep on, and I was jumping up and down on it, screaming and yelling. "Sonofabitch, come here and get me out of here!"

And the guy next to me says, "Hey, you over there." So I looked around and saw this real old guy, a little drunked up. He said, "Yeah, you're just like me. You're nothing but a bum."

Nobody ever told me that before, that I was a bum, that I was nothing. So I said, shit, I don't want to end up like this for the rest of my life.

That made me think. Here's this old drunken bum, and he sees me as his brother. Was that really the way people looked at me? But I thought I could be better, so that's where I had the edge. I believed I could do something.

—Lyle

"Lawrence was a football power at that time. It's not anymore but it was then. And Jack Martilotta recruited everybody he thought could play. He came to me when I was still in eighth grade and said, 'We want you out for football.'

"Paul Mulberg, who was the junior high school coach then, had already asked me to play football, and I told Mulberg to stick his football up his ass. I didn't want to play. I wanted to be a boxer, not a damn football player.

"So Jack Martilotta came to see me after he heard what I had told Mulberg. Black Jack. He had his black trench coat on, trying to be a rough guy. He walked over and said, 'Get your little ass out there.' So I said, 'Hell, here's some grown-up telling me. I might as well.' I got out there and played. He made a lasting impression on me.

"Sports just seemed like a waste of my time. Until I was introduced to football in the ninth grade, I didn't like it. I didn't want to play. I was terrible. I just wanted to fight—to box or do something like that.

"The other person who helped me decide to go out for football was my older brother, Peter. A tremendous athlete. Ran track, played football, played a lot of things. I looked up to him a lot, and he told me about Jack Martilotta. He told me Jack could do anything for you, would help you anytime you wanted him to.

"By the time I was in ninth grade I had met Jack Martilotta. He came to the school and talked to me because I was in a lot of trouble—I think I had just been suspended from junior high school for the sixth or seventh time—so he figured he would come over and talk to me.

"They put me at halfback. After two days of halfback, Mulberg comes over and puts his arm around me and I thought I had done something good.

He says, 'Lyle, never in my life have I ever seen a worse halfback. You are by far the worst halfback in the entire world.'

"So Mulberg said, 'Okay, I'm gonna put you at wide receiver.' He puts me at wide receiver. I go there for two days, catch one or two passes. He puts his arm around me the next week and says, 'Lyle, you are by far the worst wide receiver I have ever seen in my life.' Then he moved me to linebacker, just turned me loose and let me go and do anything I wanted to do.

"So I was a linebacker for Lawrence Junior High School, just like that. I was about 175 or 180 pounds, 6-1 tall, 15 years old.

"I liked it because he let me roam, let me go. I could just hit anybody, just go crazy. And then he told me that—because I was so big and so quick—he would move me to defensive end. He moved me to defensive end, and that's where I stayed."

Sports at Lawrence High School meant instant recognition. Those were the golden years for Lawrence athletics. Jack Martilotta was turning out an incredible series of football machines, and in track and field, Irv "Moon" Mondschein was launching a coaching career that would propel him up to the University of Pennsylvania and the big time.

A former U.S. Olympic decathlon star and outstanding end for NYU in the late 1940s, Mondschein was no less diligent in his pursuit of talent than Martilotta. And when a prospect like Alzado came along, both coaches rubbed their hands. The kid was big, and strong—and mean.

As Mondschein once said: "Give me a kid who knows what it's like to eat potato soup seven days a week." But there were lots of tough kids. It was Alzado's increcible speed that made him something special.

"It's just luck that I'm fast, just the right genes. My dad was fast with his hands and feet, but my brother

Lawrence High: Roughneck on the Gridiron

Peter... I'm gonna tell you the story. My brother Peter ran a 46-flat 440, and a 20.9, 220. He beat John Carlos in a 220 in Downing Stadium, that place under the Triborough Bridge. One of those big high school meets, the Mayor's Meet maybe.

"You know what my brother used to do? He used to line up at the end of the block and give me like a 15-, 20-yard head start. We'd run like 200 yards up the road in sneakers. All the kids in the neighborhood would say, 'Alzado's younger brother is challenging Peter,' you know? So everybody would be saying, 'Come on Lyle, come on Lyle!' Peter would give me a head start and I would just tear out, but my brother would just go like a shot and pass me up and beat me. And you know what? I never, ever beat him.

"I ran track in high school. Irv Mondschein got me out for track, 'Moon' Mondschein. My kind of coach. If you were fast, he would race you. He'd compete in anything against you.

"He went to our high school gym once. We had a high jumper, Craig Martin, who high-jumped like 6 feet 5 inches. Irv Mondschein went in there and jumped 6-6. *He was 40 years old.*

"Mondschein was the first man who ever slapped my face. I never retaliated. It was when I was out for football in tenth grade. He was the assistant coach to J. C. Hillen, who was my head coach on the junior varsity.

"One day Moon said, 'I want you out for track.' I looked at him like, who are you? A guy like Martilotta would say, 'Hey Lyle, why don't you come on out? C'mon, it'll be good for you.' But Moon says, 'I want you out for track. Get your ass dressed. You're out for track.' I said to myself anyone who can talk to me like that, I'm getting out there. So I went out for track and I developed, I learned how to run. He taught me how to run, how to control my body and my movements. He built strength in my legs.

"I can remember one day, one of the first weeks I was out there, we ran around the entire school, like 800 yards around the entire school. There was a door that some of the athletes would cut through because they didn't want to run. So I said, shit, I'm gonna cut through too. Moon saw me, but I didn't know he saw me. So I go out the other door and I finish the race—with one of my best times ever—and he walked over to me, looked at me, and then he slapped me. 'If you ever cheat me again,' he said, 'I'll never ever help you to do anything.'

"So from then on in I learned, I studied, and I worked hard. I ended up running the 100 against Uniondale my senior year, and my best time was 9.9. I led off the 880 relay, and my best time out of the blocks was 21.9. I ran the 440 in 49.5. My best broad jump was 23 feet 1 inch.

"There are great stories about how Mondschein loved to compete against guys on the team. Like, we had a guy, Jerry Valentine, who ran the 100 in about 9.6. And I'll never forget the time Moon said, "Okay, you guys! You gonna fool around, I'll tell you what. You run this practice for me if I beat you out of the start. Jerry said, 'Does this go for everybody?' 'Everybody,' Moon said. So they get down there, and Zack Watson says, 'Runners take your mark, set, powww!' Moon killed him. Left him standing in the blocks. It was a ten-yard race. Moon just left him. I was in awe of the man. I respect him as much as I respect anybody.

"You could say, thanks to my dad I've got genes that let you run fast, and maybe I should be thankful to him, but then I remember that he tried to destroy my family. I hate him for that.

"And sometimes I think, what if I'd been born a guy with feet turned in, 5-3, 108 pounds, couldn't run fast, thick glasses? It's possible, you know. God pulls the ticket out, and that's you. I think about it, but not very

Lawrence High: Roughneck on the Gridiron

often, because I don't want to say, 'Gosh, what if I were this, or what if I were that?' If I were seven feet tall I'd be playing basketball.

"One important thing I've learned: don't forget the people you meet on the way up, 'cause I know that, when I'm down and can't play anymore, I'm gonna pass those same people. They may look at me differently, but I won't forget them. And I don't forget people who've been true friends to me, people like Mark Lyons, my wife Sharon—number one—and Richie Mollo, Sal Ciampi, Ira Gordon, Larry Schepps, Irv Mondschein, Jack Martilotta. They've been good to me."

"The most significant friendships of Alzado's life were formed at Lawrence. Gordon, Schepps, and Lyons were teammates on the football team. Mollo had gone on to stardom at Virginia Tech. Ciampi was a legend who returned. One of the great linebackers in Lawrence history, Ciampi went on to star on the Bob Griese teams at Purdue. Then he came back to coach at Lawrence, when Alzado was first getting into football. He has achieved recent notoriety through Alzado's emergence as a national celebrity.

"Sal must be going bananas right now. 'I see my name in *Sports Illustrated*, Lyle. I turn around and I hear that you got knifed. What are you doing? You're making me nervous.'

"In the fall I played defensive end, and Jack Martilotta used to tell me, 'Lyle, I want you to go get that quarterback. I don't care who's in your way, you get him.' So that's what I did. He just turned me loose.

"I was a street-fighter type. I didn't have any techniques, didn't learn any until I came to Denver. I'd just run over people, run around them, anything I could. Punch 'em, slap 'em.

"Lawrence played in what we called the Black and Blue Division—Freeport, Hempstead, East Meadow, Massapequa, Berner, Lawrence, Uniondale—vicious football. Of course, I look back on it, and at that time it was tremendous. I thought no one in the world could beat Lawrence High School.

"The guys I played with all ended up drinking wine and selling dope, on dope, in jail, killing each other off. But I'll tell you something, some of the finest athletes in the United States are coming out of that area. I can go down the list of names and tell you the things they've done, and you won't believe it. John Wilson—the National Freshman Shot-Put Record Holder—is in the Peace Corps. He quit high school to join the Peace Corps. Elliott Fortune ran the 100 in 9.7; Craig Martin, the New York State Hurdle Champion, ran the 220 in 22 flat. Go down the line. The athletes who went to Lawrence High School were gifted. On all-around gifts, I was down the list."

Weight training on a supervised basis was almost unknown in the high school programs of the 1960s, but it was at Lawrence that Alzado realized the need for added strength. He was running into a new obstacle, the double-team block: teams would leave their tight end in to help the offensive tackle with him. Sometimes they'd use a running back to pick him up if he managed to beat the double team.

To combat that, he turned to weight lifting to increase his upper-body strength. The precedent had been set by Sal Ciampi and Richie Mollo.

"I used to lift weights in Richie Mollo's father's garage. Big John Mollo. Big John was about 5-9 and about 400 pounds. *Big* John! He had a garage, and he got dumbbells for us—you know, weights or something. Sal and Richie graduated together. Sal was All-American at Purdue, Richie was All-American at Virginia Tech, and they would lift weights. They would list the records in chalk on the wall of the garage. When we got there—me and Mark Lyons—we would go into the weight room, break their records, and erase their marks. And every time we broke one, we would call and say, 'Hey, we erased another one of your records today.'

"What else did we do to get in shape?... We used to pick up garbage, for Inwood Sanitation. Everybody did it—Richie, Sal—so of course Mark and I did that. And we used to run behind the trucks with our ankle weights and body weights on. They'd go five miles an hour and we'd jog behind them and pick up the garbage. People at school would ask me what I did during the summer, and I told 'em I was a garbiologist.

"Lemme tell you about our teams at Lawrence. We were 8-0 and 7-2 in the two years I played varsity. I made an All-County team my senior year—never All-State or anything like that, but All-County was enough, you know?

"We lost to Berner, 18-12, and that was a big thing because Lawrence was really a powerhouse in those days. People were scared to play us. We just got outcoached, that's all. And now we were ready to play Mount Vernon, the monsters of Westchester County.

"Mount Vernon had won two games in a row and was undefeated the year before. They came in two Greyhound buses they had, like Michigan State, with 'Mount Vernon' written on them. They came off the bus in a single file, ran all the way around the football field in a single line, and ended up on the other end. We looked at these guys, and they were massive. I thought we were playing Michigan State, and in the '60s Michigan State was a powerhouse. But we went out and beat them, 20 to 17. That was one of the hardest football games I ever played in high school. It was just vicious.

"I remember a little halfback of theirs named Warren—a Little All-American at Bridgeport—but most of all I remember they were big and it said 'Mount Vernon,' M-O-U-N-T V-E-R-N-O-N, written on their chests. It was one of my better games, but I don't remember the statistics now. I got the quarterback three or four times, punched people... My typical high school game.

"We were the Black and Blue Division, the melting pot. We played Massapequa, the Italians from East Meadow, and the blacks from Berner. And then, in my junior year, they set up a game between Lawrence High School and Hewlett High School—all the rich kids, all the things we couldn't stand, all the things we didn't like. The game was built up incredibly. They'd won five or six games or so, they weren't too bad. We went to Hewlett and sat in this little locker room, and I'll never forget what Mr. Martilotta told us. We sat there before we went out there for the game, and he said, 'You know something, you guys? Do you know why all those people are out there looking at you, waiting for this game? They're waiting for you guys to get beat, 'cause they don't care about you, they don't care who you are. You don't have any money, you don't have anything, and they want to destroy the little you have left—and that's your pride in the athletic program Lawrence High School has.' And he had us flying. I mean we would have beaten the Los Angeles Rams that day. We went out onto that field and we beat Hewlett, 13 to 0. They had total offensive yardage minus-25 yards. We had rolled up 400-something in total offense. We had three touchdowns called back, and we knocked four or five of their players out.

"Coach Martilotta coached us on emotion. He dug down inside us, dug for our pride and dug for what really meant more to us than anything. That's the guts Lawrence High School's athletic program taught us to have.

"The crowd for that game was unbelievable. People were parked all over. I would say there were 30,000 people there. Long Island football, you generally get five or six thousand, and that's good. And I'll never forget: we all went to church together that morning, and it was just amazing. I'll never forget it."

Lawrence High: Roughneck on the Gridiron

• • •

They'd turned out in droves to see Lawrence play Hewlett, and in similar fashion Lyle Alzado's friends turned out to support him at the Super Bowl. A trio arrived Friday night and had to hustle for a place to stay, finally booking into a dorm at Tulane: Mark Lyons, Ira Gordon, and Larry Schepps—the guys from high school. Lyle's old buddies.

Ira Gordon—tall, quiet, good-looking, light-haired and light-bearded—is a health-ed teacher and freshman football coach at Great Neck, Long Island, High School. Larry Schepps is a podiatrist in Fort Lauderdale. Mark Lyons is the head football coach at Stamford, Connecticut, High. The violence of their past is not reflected in their professions. The Dead End Kids have gone straight.

MARK LYONS

Dark-haired, sharp-featured, with darting black eyes, Lyons talked about the early days of his friendship with Lyle Alzado.

"We met in junior high and hit it off right away," Mark recalls. "We're still like brothers. He was best man at my wedding, and I was his. I guess, looking back, there was no way we wouldn't have been close. Our families were about the same—mixed up—and we sort of took care of each other, always hung together.

"He was a tall, thin kid in his junior year, no upperbody size at all. But he was dedicated, man, the most tremendously dedicated kid I ever knew. He wanted to make it in sports. It was a way out, a way to get esteem. We'd go to parties and I'd have a beer, a couple drinks, but Lyle would bring along a quart of milk. *Milk*. He was a real individual, and he didn't care what anybody thought. He drank milk.

"Nobody called him a sissy. He got—*we* got—in a lot of fights. We came from the other side of the tracks, and I know I had an inferiority complex growing up. Maybe Lyle did too, but we were determined to get esteem through sports. I was going to play baseball for the Yankees and Lyle was going to the Giants in football.

"Well, after our junior football season we made this pact that we were going to go unbeaten as seniors. We'd become Somebody. We made this pact that nobody was going to beat our football team, and then we went against Berner in our first game and it was raining like hell. We had dedicated our whole lives and we lost. There went our undefeated season. So, we got in my old beat-up 1952 Plymouth and cried our eyes out for two, three hours.

"We felt dead, ruined, but we decided to make another pact—that we wouldn't lose again and that we'd win the championship. We won the rest of our games, and our success seemed to do something to our whole school. That year we won every championship in our league—baseball, track, basketball, everything.

"Lyle was super in track. He could run the 100 in 9.9, but we had four kids faster than that. He never threw the shot because we had old John Wilson—a 360 pounder—who could throw the thing 65 feet. And Lyle could box—man, could he fight! He used to take two pair of boxing gloves to Atlantic Beach, sneak under the fence, draw a ring in the sand, and challenge the lifeguards. Lyle was only 16 then, and he had this skinny upper body, but he'd challenge these 25-, 26-year-old well-built guys. I told him he was crazy, that he'd get killed, but he never did. Once he took on this lifeguard who was an ex-Marine, a tough-looking guy, and Lyle beat the hell out of the guy. Lyle could have been a world-class boxer, and that's not just me getting carried away because he's my friend. He has speed, punch, stamina, and that killer instinct. He never lost.

"We worked hard to get in shape, though, probably harder than anybody. In the summer before our senior year, we worked on a garbage truck and would get through about noon. But we couldn't get back in the yard until one, so Lyle and me would strap on these 20-pound weight vests and jog behind the truck as it went slow, to kill time. Then we'd go to the high school and lift weights, then off to Richie Mollo's house in Woodmere to lift some more.

"Richie was our idol then, along with Sal Ciampi. They were the big football players in our school—the guys who made it to college—and we wanted to be like 'em. Anyway, Richie had this gym in his garage, and we just kept up the old tradition of lifting weights in Mollo's garage. We had this chart, and we would go for records. When we broke Sal's or Richie's records, we'd go crazy. We'd tell Mrs. Mollo, the neighbor kids, the dogs, and then we'd call Richie and Sal and tell them another of their records had gone down.

"Lyle could bench-press almost 500 pounds, but we had to recruit kids to lift the weight up for him so he could do it. We didn't have any fancy benches.

"Anyway, Lyle dedicated his whole life to becoming successful. He was going to play for the Giants, and I was going to play baseball. I was a prospect, too, but I got hurt. I didn't have the body Lyle had, and just couldn't make it. We both feel we've been successful in our way—maybe not from a material standpoint, but I have the respect of the community I live in, and look what Lyle has accomplished.

"I always knew he'd make it but there were times when... Well, when it was my birthday one time, we decided to go out and have some fun. We met these girls, and they took us over to a ritzy place on the North Shore. There was Lyle, myself, Ira Gordon, and Larry Schepps. Lyle had bought me this shirt for my birthday. He had saved money from the job on the garbage truck, and he felt pretty good about the shirt. So I wore it.

"Naturally, we got in a fight with these guys in the bar. And I swear, one of them was 6 feet 10—I mean it, 6-10—and he ripped my shirt. That's all Lyle had to see. But the guy was so tall Lyle couldn't hit him in the jaw. So Lyle got up on this chair and laid the guy out. Most of the guys in the place took off, and we got the hell out, too.

Lyle used to come to the bars with us, but he hardly ever drank. He didn't really start until after his first year at Yankton, and only then because the coach there told him beer had protein and protein was good for him. All I know is, he went off to college at 200 pounds and came back that summer at 230. He said it was the beer.

"We did some drinking after he graduated and was drafted by the Broncos. I think he had been with them a year, because it was after his rookie reason. We decided to go to the Osprey Bar in Manasquan, New Jersey. It was supposed to be the longest in the world, and we were going to find out. I had about 400 bucks and Lyle had around 800. Anyway, we walked in in our bathing suits, and Lyle was wearing this mask. He said he wanted to buy everybody in the place a drink. Then he went crazy and started dancing on the bar, and everybody was singing and having a hell of a time. It cost us about 300 bucks to buy for the bar, but there are guys who were there who still talk about Lyle.

We also went to this other place in Jersey, called DJ's, and where Lyle went in and ordered 200 beers and had the bartender line 'em up four deep. Then he started pouring 'em over people's heads. It was the greatest weedend you'd ever want to see. Except maybe for this one in New Orleans. Lyle sent me tickets, and I'm going to be there tomorrow to see the Broncos beat Dallas. I wouldn't miss it for anything."

Lawrence High: Roughneck on the Gridiron

LARRY SCHEPPS

On Saturday, the day before the Super Bowl, Larry Schepps dropped over at the Sheraton, the Broncos' hotel, to pay a short visit.

"I'll just say hello," he said. "Lyle won't want to see anybody today. He'll be thinking about the game, getting himself ready... you know."

He studied his fingers a moment, then smiled.

"Watch Lyle tomorrow," he said. "Watch his fingers, the second and third fingers of each hand. Before the game he'll be rubbing them together, twitching them almost. Watch his head. He'll be bobbing it up and down, like a horse."

"How the hell do you know that?" someone asked him, and he smiled again.

"I just know," Larry Schepps said.

He is well-dressed, stocky, sandy-haired, and good-looking. He is 5-10, 190 pounds, the same size as when he played the other defensive end—across from Lyle—at Lawrence High. He looks exactly like what he is, a successful Jewish doctor, a podiatrist with a brand-new practice in Fort Lauderdale.

"For three years Larry Schepps went into hiding while he was studying to be a doctor," Alzado once said. "We didn't see him, then next time he came around, he'd made it."

You look carefully at Larry Schepps' face—scar near the left eye, nose slightly bent—and you figure that maybe this is a guy who knows how to use his fists.

Larry Schepps, the son of a fairly well-to-do produce distributor in Long Island, could always handle himself in a fight. But when he met Lyle Alzado and began hanging around with him, he stepped up a notch in competition. He was a charter member of the Immortal Five—Alzado, Mark Lyons, Ira Gordon, Richie Mollo, and Schepps—the five hard guys of Nassau County.

On Saturday night, the night before Super Bowl XII, Larry Schepps nursed a beer along and talked about the old days:

"I'm sure right now Lyle is up in his room, cocking his neck up and down, twitching his fingers, and getting ready for Ralph Neely. He's always had that little mannerism, that little twitch. I think he developed the twitch with his fingers to get himself ready for action; before a fight they were like antennae, maybe like lobster claws. Every time he was about to get into a fight, like when he was a bouncer in a discotheque, I'd look at him and see his neck start going back and forth. Then he'd start grunting, like hrumm, hrumm. And his fingers—his second and third fingers on both hands—would start rubbing against each other. They were like antennae. I knew from that moment on, you'd better get out of the way because he was coming after you.

"When he talks about the Cowboys I see him doing that. Just before he goes in for a series his fingers will be moving, his head will be bobbing, and believe me, they'll be in for it. I don't mean just Ralph Neely, I mean the whole team. He will literally take on half the side of the Dallas team.

"I think he's getting to the point where other people are just scared to play against him. He didn't have a great game against Art Shell in the playoffs because I think *Shell* posed a threat to Lyle, not so much the Oakland Raiders. He got psyched up for the fight against the Oakland Raiders, but he got too involved with Art Shell, and it was just like two gladiators going at it in an arena. They were out to destroy each other, and because of that I don't think he played the best game.

"But against Ralph Neely... Well, Neely doesn't pose the same kind of threat to Lyle as Art Shell does. He's not 320 pounds coming at you 50 miles per hour like a locomotive. I don't think Lyle will mess too much with Ralph Neely; he'll just keep him away from him, play a lot better, and get to the quarterback a lot more. His pursuit down the line will even be quicker. There won't be any wild forearms, fists, and spitting being carried on with Ralph Neely.

"Lyle is sort of like Muhammad Ali: he psyches his man out, and he says he does a lot of things, like spitting. I never saw him spit at anybody on the field, although if he says he did it, he probably did. I don't think Lyle was the type of guy who had to stab anyone. He did his stabbing with his hands. My experience was that Lyle Alzado could take care of *anyone* with his two hands. He never needed any iron or any other implement.

"I never saw him lose a fight. If there were three or four guys coming at him, he'd always have his back to a wall. He had this sixth sense that a fighter always has. He just knew where to be when he was having a fight, and I think it's the same way he is on a football field. He knows where to be when the guys are running the ball against him.

"I was always a good fighter to start with, but anytime you went with Lyle Alzado, you knew you were getting into a fight. In fact, one summer I was in bed for two months with mononucleosis. After two months, my parents let me out of the house with Lyle, because they felt Lyle was a safe guy to hang around with; they felt nothing would happen to me hanging around with Lyle. Little did they know. We went to a disco out in Great Neck. They imported their biggest guy in Great Neck, and he was 6-10, All-County in basketball, and he came through those doors like King Kong. It was Mark Lyons, myself, Ira Gordon, and Lyle, just taking on the whole place. There must have been $2,000 worth of damages. I had a chair broken over my head, and I wasn't feeling too good anyway after two months with mono. Lyle would never hear of anyone laying a hand on me, taking advantage of me, though, and the guy who broke the chair over my head—Lyle just broke him in half.

"The 6-10 guy had a chunk of jaw removed from his chin. I'll never forget it. It was a disco with a kitchen in the back, and when this guy came at Lyle, Lyle just pounded the guy right into the kitchen, through the swinging doors onto the kitchen table where they kept the pots. After the fight was over I saw this huge wedge of skin hanging out of the guy's jaw. It was just unbelievable.

"To make it worse, not only did Lyle cause the place $2,000 worth of damages, but he asked for his money back! It had cost $5 to get into the place, and we had to lend him the money. Lyle was so annoyed about them throwing him out that he asked the bouncer for his $5 back. And you better believe the bouncer gave the money back to him. That was the most unbelievable thing. It's not so much that he came out on top in the fight—I knew he'd do that—but after causing all the damage in there he had the nerve to ask the guy for his $5 back.

"Why did Lyle fight so much? I think it was the Darwin theory of survival of the fittest. And I think when Lyle is out on that field he views football as survival of the fittest. He never had decent food on his table, and he's fighting for the food; he's fighting for his wife and family.

"Nowadays when he gets out of the football uniform, he doesn't think of survival the same way he used to. People don't pose a threat to him, and he's a very sensitive guy who loves to help people. But in his way he always loved people. When we grew up in Lawrence, we used to go to the town diner at night, and Lyle could only afford to have these hash-brown potatoes which were a quarter while everyone else was

Lawrence High: Roughneck on the Gridiron   45

eating hamburgers and sandwiches at 12 o'clock at night. Lyle was the most popular guy there, and the most affluent girls always wanted to go out with him because he was the most exciting person to go out with. And they didn't care what their parents thought of Lyle Alzado. They didn't mind eating hash-browns and having milk.

"We used to go to parties all the time and they'd say to us—to me and Ira and Mark—'What would you like?' We'd say, 'Oh, we'll have a beer.' Then they'd say, 'Lyle, what would you like?' and he'd say, 'I'll have a glass of milk.' And these mothers, the mothers of the kids throwing the party, were just so impressed with this enormous guy drinking milk, that they all loved him. And he never had any enemies except guys who wanted to try him out.

"In football... well, we had bigger guys on the team, but Lyle was just an aggressive man-eater. He didn't have many techniques, just straight brutal force and a great pride for the team. He was a street-fighter type on the field; I don't think there was a game where he got off the field without blowing on his hands. At Elmont he knocked two quarterbacks out of the game.

"I grew up in Brooklyn, and I was 13 when I moved out to the Island. I didn't know anyone until I met Lyle, who was the first guy to come over and introduce himself to me. And after that, once I became friends with him, I never had any trouble from anybody.

"He had a reputation even then. I remember the time we went to Nathan's and he kicked over two motorcycles which belonged to a subsidiary of Hell's Angels. They didn't do a thing about it. Lyle was like Wyatt Earp. People felt like they had to test him. And anytime we went to town or to a disco, they'd import their strongest guy in the neighborhood; it always turned into a brawl, it usually involved Mark Lyons, Ira Gordon, Lyle and me, and it was always four against four. But we were always on the winning side. I hardly ever got hit when he was around.

"I first met Lyle on the opening day of football practice at Lawrence Junior High. After practice I had gotten into a fight, and I beat the hell out of this guy, and Lyle came over to me and said, 'Hey, my name is Lyle Alzado. Let's be friends. And he invited me over to his house that night.

"I lived in a pretty affluent section of Lawrence, and I didn't know what to think, coming over to this guy's house. He had a huge house like you see on *The Munsters*, but it had almost nothing in it but piled-up furniture in the bathroom. It was a really scary-looking old house. It was all torn apart.

His father was a junk collector; in fact, we used to call him Warehouse Pat, because their place was a total warehouse. He had old boats in the yard; he had six or seven jalopies; he had old trucks; and he usually had a donkey tied to a pole in the back. He was just like a junk collector.

"His father was a really strange dude. He was always half-loaded, and he owned a bar in Inwood called the Golden Dream. It wasn't doing too well, so he started serving drinks to kids 13, 14, 15... The bar became a spectacular success overnight. Lyle was the bouncer. It became spectacular, but then the cops came down on him and that was the end of the Golden Dream.

His father was a very tough guy, a real fighter. You wouldn't want to mess with his father. His nose was pushed to one side; he always smelled from alcohol, and you just didn't want to get near the guy.

"The Alzados lived on sugar, milk, and bread. I would go over there with Ira on a Friday night, and that's all they'd be eating—bread, milk, and sugar. It was just incredible. That's all you'd ever find in the refrigerator. And I don't mean *one* container of milk, I mean just totally *packed* with quarts of milk and bread and sugar. Nothing else.

"Ira, his father, Lyle, and I used to go to the Giant

games. Lyle didn't really care who won the game, he just stared down at the guys on the field. He'd look at them and say to Ira or myself, '77,' or '84,' or '39'... How big is that guy?'

"And we'd look in the program and say, '6-2, 240, Lyle.' He'd make this slight grunt, cock his head back, then he'd just start dreaming.

"He was always dreaming about getting bigger—about getting bigger, faster, and more hostile every day. And I think he'd have been 6 feet tall, 190 to 210 pounds, but he was always dreaming. And instead of reaching his goal—his goal I'm sure would have been 6-7, 290—he ended up at 6-3, 255.

"I really believe the power of his mind motivated his body to keep growing. It was an amazing thing: he weighed 195 pounds when he left high school, and stood about 6-1. The following year, when he came back from college where they'd given him something to eat—which he never really had at home—he was 6-3, 230. He just never stopped dreaming until he got where he wanted to be.

"Lyle was always an impressive football player, due to his sheer killer instinct. He could definitely turn a game around anytime he wanted. He rushed on every play; he never respected the run; he always came after the quarterback, every play. And it was very rare to see the same quarterback who started the game finish it.

"In Elmont we were playing for the high school championship of District Two in Long Island. Elmont had a super quarterback and a great tight end, and that combination could have destroyed us. But Lyle knocked the first-, second-, and third-string quarterbacks out of the game. He demolished the total quarterback situation for Elmont, and they couldn't do much after that.

"Head-to-head match-ups always happened on our team. The other team always had their best, biggest, strongest player playing against Lyle, and they always went at it either before the play, during the play, after the play, or after the game. Freeport had this big dude playing for them. He was All-County, and before the game Lyle started mentally meditating, getting himself psyched up—not so much for the game but for the fight he was going to have with this guy. And they went at it during the first quarter. And once Lyle had beat the hell out of him, we won the game.

"At one halftime, when we were losing 21-0 to Long Beach, Coach Martilotta came in and said, 'Big tough Alzado, big tough Alzado.' He said, 'Lyle, how many guys on you?'

"Lyle said, 'Two guys.'

"Then he said to me, 'How many guys on you, Larry?'

"And I said, 'There's two guys on me.'

"He went through the whole defensive line like that and then said, 'Well, I just added that up. There must be 22 guys playing offense for Long Beach.'

"But, really, the way he got us to turn around that game was by picking on Lyle. He picked up a blackboard and just threw it right at Lyle, yelling, 'Big tough Alzado, big tough Alzado.' Lyle started crying, he was so infuriated. When he went out on the field I was so sure he was going to tear the goalpost down, I got scared myself.

"At the opening kickoff of the second half, Craig Marton ran the ball back 97 yards, and then we got on defense.

"By the end of the game Long Beach had lost their halfback, their quarterback, half the offensive guys on the team. Lyle was just destroying them. And when he came off the field at the end of the game, he was just bleeding all over the place.

"The final score was 27-21. We won the game, and no one ever made fun of Lyle again. Coach Martilotta never came over to him and said, 'Big tough Alzado.' I think he was frightened by what he had done.

Lawrence High: Roughneck on the Gridiron

"I guess you've heard about Lyle's record as a boxer. Believe me, he could have been a great one, if the idea of it hadn't upset his mother so much.

"I remember my uncle's friend in Lawrence knew Rocky Graziano, and one day Lyle, Mark Lyons, Ira, and I went down to my uncle's house and Rocky Graziano was there. They had this heavy bag, and Lyle started hitting it. Graziano's eyes just kept getting bigger and bigger. Lyle kept on hitting the bag harder and harder, and Rocky Graziano was just going crazy. Finally he brought Lyle over to the corner. He said, 'Listen, I want you to do something for me. I want you to come down to this place in East New York. I want to see what you can do.' They got Lyle a match with this guy who was ranked tenth in the world. I don't know the guy's name, but he was ranked tenth. And they went over to the guy's corner and said to him, 'Listen, this is just a young kid; he's 18 years old. He's only boxed in the boys' athletic club, so don't hit him too hard. We just want to see what he has.'

"They went at it for one or two rounds, and pretty soon both of them were really getting into it. When it was over they went to this boxer and said, 'What do you think of Lyle?' The guy said, 'Well, as hard as I hit him, he hit me harder.' I mean Lyle just whipped the guy. And Rocky Graziano pleaded with Lyle to quit football and start boxing.

"But Lyle's mother would never hear of it, since his father had been a boxer and he turned into a bum. So Lyle had to go another way in life, and he chose football.

"You can imagine what Lyle and the rest of us must have been like in high school. We were the storm troopers, and we kept everyone in line—actually, Lyle kept everyone in line in that school. There were a lot of race riots after we left, but those things never happened when Lyle was around. He kept things in control. He was very good in black-white relations. Black guys always respected him because he was a fighter and he never BS'd them.

"Lyle used to work for my father two months in the summer. My father put him on these trucks—loaded with onions and celery from California and rice from the Far East—and he'd have Lyle unloading the trucks by himself. Each celery crate weighed from 50 to 75 pounds, but Lyle never minded because he was building himself up. You didn't even have to pay him to unload trucks; he liked it because it was making him stronger. Anyway, my dad paid him $20 a day. Lyle always gave it to his mother, so sometimes my father would slip him $5—just so he'd have some money in his pocket.

"Dad sort of took care of him that way. We'd have him over for dinner. I remember one time my mother prepared three chickens: two for Lyle and one for the family.

"Lyle considered himself Jewish when we were growing up because there were so many Jewish kids around. I think he really wanted to fit in, religionwise, but then again the guys that we hung around with weren't Jewish. We hung around with the tough guys.

"I'll never forget the time Ira and I went to this party in Hewlett Harbor, a rich kids' party thrown by the Hewlett basketball players. We had busted into the party, and they threw us out and threatened us. So we went back to another party where the poor kids were hanging out, where Lyle and his crew were. (Ira and I could always cross the lines because we lived in the affluent neighborhood, but we always chose to hang around with Lyle.)

"Lyle would never hear of any of his friends getting thrown out of a party, so he came over. He had this friend who owned a taxicab, and he piled all of us in, and took us down there, then he challenged the whole place. Four or five guys came at him—it was the most unbelievable thing.

Lawrence High: Roughneck on the Gridiron

"All you could see were guys just flying in the air and Lyle Alzado with his back to the wall. He beat the hell out of all those guys. It was a real debutante party, and there were all these guys with blood all over their tuxedos and everything. But it wasn't enough for Lyle to beat up guys; he always had to have the last word.

"They called the police, but Lyle had this knack for evading the police. Here's a guy who was a real street fighter, but he had a good sense of knowing what to do. He turned his jacket inside out that night—he was wearing his Lawrence jacket—and he made himself fit right into the dark. We got away from the police.

"But before the police came—and after he beat up all those guys—it was not enough for Lyle to destroy the party. He was hungry. They were serving chicken at that party, so he had a few pieces of chicken. After he ate his chicken he said, 'Any more?' Nobody said anything, so he just walked out.

"He's like a modern gunslinger, a modern legend in Long Island. He *was* the legend, and still *is* the legend. They used to call him Animal Lyle Alzado—Animal Alzado. But I'll tell you, in many ways my life has been worth the living because Lyle was always my friend, because people around us—the kids who drove to school in their father's Cadillacs and Eldorados and Lincolns—never thought Lyle Alzado would make it. He's not only made it, he's made it across the country. Everyone knows about him—as a human being and as a really great football player.

"And he knew he was going to make it. In fact, after our last football game—it was a crazy thing that night—he just had to go back to the field at Lawrence High School. He climbed over the 10-foot fence, walked down to the field, and he said good-bye to it. And from that day on I said, this guy is definitely destined to make it. I never saw anyone say good-bye to a field like that.

"The amazing thing about the friendship between

the four or five of us was that people would never invite us to parties with Lyle because they thought we were a bunch of ruffians. They figured we were going to destroy the party and get into fights. People wouldn't accept us. But these little rich kids who drove around in their father's Lincolns and played poker for $150 a hand, they really never amounted to anything. Lyle's friends are the people who amounted to something, and that says a lot for our little group—a group of people everyone thought was just too rough to associate with."

SAL CIAMPI

Sal Ciampi is 5-9, 196 pounds—13 pounds down from his playing weight at Purdue, where he had a reputation as a tough, hard-nosed little linebacker who wasn't afraid to mix it up. In 1961 he led Lawrence to the Rutgers Cup—best high school team in Nassau County—and won the Thorpe Award for best all-around player. The Thorpe carried a gaudy assortment of former winners: Jimmy Brown, Matt Snell, Paul Rochester, etc.

He co-captained Purdue, along with former Giant guard Jerry Shay, then came back to coach at Lawrence. He met Alzado there, and remembers him as a willing student of football—but a rough one.

Ciampi remembers: "I was a high school senior; Lyle was in the eighth grade. We used to pal around with Mark Lyons, who's still his best friend. They were always real close. But those kids idolized football players. I came home from Purdue, back to coach at Lawrence, and I see this kid Lyle—big and strong. I was from the Big-Ten, and not many kids from Inwood

Lawrence High: Roughneck on the Gridiron

ever went to collegiate football. Oh, they'd go to school, but hardly any finished; people from Inwood generally ended up working for the people in the Five Towns area. My father drove a sanitation truck; other parents were gardeners and servants for the people in places like Lawrence, Hewlett, Cedarhurst, and Woodmere.

"We had so many good ballplayers, but they just never seemed to stick it out in college. I graduated from Purdue and played in the Blue-Gray All-Star game in Montgomery, Alabama, in 1965. Christmas Day—the game was on national television, and when I came home it was like being a returning hero: people met me at the airport.

"When I went back to the school, I saw Lyle. He was so much bigger than the kid I'd known before, and real tough. I was all set to go back to Purdue for my master's, but Irv Mondschein called me, asking if I'd come back to Lawrence to coach.

"I took the job, coaching jayvee. Lyle was a senior by then, very raw, but an aggressive player on defense. On offense, he didn't know how to block. I used to go out early to work with him, but he didn't have the temperament to be an offensive lineman, a blocker. He didn't want to block people; he just wanted to get out there and slug them around.

"The summer before Lyle went to college, I got out the sleds and worked on techniques with him: defense, basic stuff, fundamentals like rolling his hips and using the forearm blow. Hell, when he played in high school all he did was go as hard as he could and hit somebody. I knew he'd have to know how to deliver a forearm blow, so we worked hard on that all summer. That's when I told him he could be as good as he wanted to be. I knew he could play at Purdue or anywhere. He was better than I was.

"Sometimes it's hard to imagine him coming out of Inwood. Maybe Inwood sounds like the kind of place where you'd get stabbed just walking down the street, but it's not really like that. It's a place where you have to work hard to get ahead. There are proud people there who work like hell, and they're proud to see somebody like Lyle—one of their own—get out there and make it.

"Lyle would probably be the same way; he's always been very emotional. I remember once, during a game, Jack told him to get the quarterback on every play. Even after the kid handed off, Lyle would chase him. In that game he drew three 15-yard penalties for chasing the quarterback right to the bench and going after him, but the quarterback was so unnerved he threw five or six interceptions. Lyle was an intense kid, a team player all the way. Except that he couldn't play offense, just didn't have the temperament for it at all.

"Once, when he came back from Yankton—6-3, 235, all muscle—he got into a basketball game in the high school gym, with five or six other kids he didn't know too well. One kid said something to him about fouling, and he put all of them against a wall. By the time he finished they were lying all over the gym or running out the doors, yelling and everything. I asked him what the hell he thought he was doing and gave him a lecture about fouling in basketball.

"He embarrassed me once, when we were clowning around in the halls. I was just out of Purdue, he was a senior in high school, and I could just throw kids around. But instead of throwing him, I ended up defending myself. I didn't want to be shown up by some high school senior after four years at Purdue.

"Everybody's so proud of him, back in Inwood. And he doesn't forget. One time when he was back for a visit, he came out to my place in East Islip. Mark Lyons was there, too. Lyle started drinking scotch and whisky. I told him he shouldn't mix that stuff; he'd get sick, and we had to drive him back to Inwood. So he took the bottle of scotch and the bottle of whisky, poured some of each in a glass, and started drinking. It was 6:30 at night, and I turned to Mark and said, 'He's gonna get sick. Let's drive him back.' So we all climbed in my Rambler and headed for Inwood with Lyle in the back. We got to Inwood and Mark and I got sick, and guess who had to drive us back to East Islip?

"One Super Bowl Sunday, Lyle was at my place, and this other guy who was there—Rocky Gilmore, five-and-a-half feet tall—started in on Lyle. Gilmore said to him, 'You can always watch the Super Bowl with us, because you ain't ever gonna be in it.' I was afraid Lyle was going to pop him, but he just said, *'We'll be in it.'* I'm so happy Denver didn't make it last year, the season Lyle was out. He'd have died if he hadn't been able to play.

"There are so many things I remember about Lyle. One of his first seasons with Denver, he said, 'Sal, I'm going to break my ass to make All-Pro.' That was when Deacon Jones was All-Pro every year. Lyle said, 'It's my dream to make All-Pro someday, but they're not even looking at me.'

"He called me before this season ended, to ask how he did. I said, 'When you finish the season, come and see me. There's a lot of work to do.' He always comes back and asks us how he did. He respects us. That's the kind of guy he is. He doesn't forget his friends, the people who helped him when he was a kid...."

JACK MARTILOTTA

He was short and stocky, and he liked to affect a hard-guy look: black beret, black trench coat. Naturally the kids at Lawrence High School started to call Jack Martilotta "Black Jack."

Black Jack was their football coach. He saved a lot

of kids from the streets, but Lyle Alzado was his crowning achievement. He didn't try to snuff out Alzado's fighting instincts; instead he channeled them onto the football field. A focal figure in Lyle's life, he even cared enough to travel to Denver to meet Lyle's plane the first time Alzado visited the Broncos.

"I'll never forget Lyle," Martilotta says. "When he was a senior, he had a hell of a pair of hands. He could have been a heavyweight boxer. Matter of fact, Rocky Graziano once called me and asked if I'd turn Alzado over to him. He said he wanted to take him on, promote him as a heavyweight.

"I said I'd talk to Lyle about it, and I did. Lyle said he'd do whatever I told him to do, but that he had a burning desire to play football. I told him to go to college, take a shot at it, see what happened. I told him he could always go into boxing if he changed his mind. So he went to Yankton, and he was so good there was no doubt about him becoming a football player.

"He was one hell of a kid, though. Never a problem. He'd work his tail off for you, and you had to *keep* him out of the gym on Sundays. He wasn't that good a football player as a junior, so I told him, 'If you really want it, you're going to have to lift weights and build yourself up.' He lifted, lifted, lifted, like an absolute animal, he was so determined.

"And you know, there was something else about him that helped him make it in football. He had a nasty streak...."

THREE:

The Fighting Greyhounds of Yankton

I weighed 290 when I got out of there. We had three offensive linemen over 265, a 265-pound defensive end, and a 250-pound middle linebacker. Our quarterback was 6-4, 220. We used to just crush people, beat them silly. It was ridiculous. They called Yankton College the Fightin' Greyhounds, but they should have called us the Elephants.

—Lyle

"You see, I never thought I was going to go to college, never planned for it. I just didn't care about studying. Passing was 65, and I was running a 55-60 average. But I went to class all the time. I'm sure some of the teachers passed me because I was always there, because I was an athlete. Sometimes they'd keep me late, try to work with me. I appreciated it, but my attention span wasn't very long. I just didn't care.

"I wanted to be a boxer. I loved to box. I started when I was 14 or 15: club fights in Police Athletic Leagues, downstairs in the gymnasium. I loved it. I was great. Joe Cannamera—he's the guy who helped me train—always matched me with the bigger guys. It was amazing. He put me in the ring with this guy who was so big and fat that I said, 'How the hell am I gonna hit this guy?' He just came swinging at me. I said the hell with him, just hit him back and knocked him out.

"I was a quick hitter. Combination puncher. My left jab was one of my better punches because I could keep people unbalanced with it. And I had a devastating right. I'd knock people out with my right hand all the time. Fair left hook. I would crank up in a fight once in a while, but mostly I would lay back and come up off the ropes. I fought best off the ropes, boy did I love coming off the ropes! And body punch—I could body-punch real well.

"I started thinking about college the beginning of my senior year in high school. That's when I started calming down a lot, when I decided I wanted to do something with my life. I had no image of college; I'd never been on a college campus, not even NYU."

The college recruiters had watched Alzado and had come away impressed. He liked the idea of the Big Ten...Purdue, where Sal Ciampi had gone, maybe Michigan State. They looked at his grades and told him to either forget it or try a junior college, where substandard grades can become respectable.

"My junior varsity coach, Mr. Hillen, had connections at New Mexico State," Alzado says, "so I was all set to go there. Then they sent a letter back saying they didn't want me. It was probably a combination of things, my grades and my record in the streets. They did some checking around and found out I'd been in jail overnight a couple of times. That must have turned them off."

He decided on Kilgore J.C. in Tyler, Texas, famous for the Kilgore Rangerettes. He was 6-1, 190, with speed. They tried him at wingback, a nifty position with one drawback: You had to be able to catch the ball.

"I couldn't catch anything," Alzado says. "I had board hands. I couldn't even catch my own hands. So they sent me home; told me I wasn't good enough to play there. I said, 'The hell with it,' and got ready to go into the service."

Coach Martilotta had other plans. He couldn't bear to see a talent like Alzado go to waste, so he called him into his office.

"Bring in all the letters you got from every school," he said. They went through them. Yankton College in Yankton, South Dakota, stood out. Little place. Peaceful. Farms and pastureland. Southeast corner of the state, 60 miles west of Sioux City, Iowa, 150 miles north of Omaha. Aggressive football recruiting campaign going on ... especially interested in Easterners. Perfect place to hide a troublesome New York kid. "Lyle," Martilotta said, "you're going to Yankton."

"I didn't know where the hell the place was. I thought it was in Alaska. I just got on the bus. I didn't tell anybody, because some of my friends would have made fun of me—the kind of guys who were jealous of anybody going to college, anybody who wouldn't end up on the corner, like them. The bus ride took 28 hours. I slept. There were only three other people on that bus.

"The place was small, very desolate, a few nice little brick houses but no building over three stories high. The gymnasium was a converted airplane hangar. The football stadium held 500. The coach, Don Birmingham, met me. Nice little guy. Young, intense. He took me into a restaurant and bought me lunch: hamburgers, milkshake, a typical New York meal. I didn't want to leave the place after that. And here's a funny thing. The place Coach Birmingham took me for lunch that first day was Kip's—owned by an uncle of the girl I eventually married.

"I got there on September 29, 1967. The team had already played two games. I had to attract attention quick, so I started fights. Pretty soon I was playing defensive end, at about 210, 220. Coach Birmingham didn't mess around. He scared me into a lot of things. One Saturday I had a lackadaisical kind of game. He just came over to me and said, 'Lyle, why don't you just turn in your uniform?' I kept the uniform, and I played like hell next game. I mean I was killing people.

"Coach Birmingham built a powerhouse out there. We went 33-4 in my four years, and were ranked nationally in the small colleges every year. The football players were from Texas, Pennsylvania, New York, North Dakota, South Dakota, all over the place. The talent was amazing. So many guys were drafted off that team... Les Goodman, Mark Herman, Chuck Smith, Chip Salvestrini, John Nielsen, Ed Clifford. And we were so big.

"My senior year, I was 290. I was in the weight room all the time, lifting enormous weights, packing the pounds on. I bench-pressed 520, did 710 in the dead lift, did a quarter-squat, and—you're not going to believe this—I quarter-squatted 1100 pounds. Made me a little dizzy. Nauseous, too. But I just kept lifting weights and eating.

"I was sitting in my room in Elm Dorm after I had eaten dinner one night, and some of the guys came over. They said, 'Lyle, why don't you represent our dorm in a pie-eating contest?' They saw how much I was eating, you know, trying to gain weight and stuff like that. I said all right, and went with them to the contest. I ate 17 pies—university and college record.

"You know who the runner-up was? Chuck Lloyd, 6-10. He was a basketball player, tenth-round draft choice of the Carolina Cougars. I'll always remember his name.

"I started three games in my freshman year. I started at middle linebacker when I was a sophomore and played fullback that year a little bit too. Best game I had I carried the ball ten times for a hundred yards. I was a straight-up-and-down runner. I took more of a beating than the tacklers did.

"The only way I could get myself in with the team, so the coaches would notice me, was to fight, so I fought with everybody. I even fought with the captain of the football team. It was unbelievable.

"First day I was out to practice with Kenny Michaelson the tight end, I went down and hit him with a forearm. He pushed me, I pushed him back, and then I started hitting him. But they noticed me, and they started playing me.

"The coach would say, 'You're crazy, what's the matter with you?' At that time I was crazy anyway, so it didn't matter. I was used to it.

"When I graduated, I was a big fat ball, but even at 290 I could run pretty well. I'd learned how to run. I could always run. But we were all big at Yankton; we used to beat people silly, used to crush people. It was just ridiculous. The offensive line was 295, 275, 265; Mike Miller—the defensive end—was 260, 265. The middle linebacker was 250. Our quarterback, Doug Cummings, was 6-4, 220. This was a collection of enormous people who couldn't get into other schools.

"We had some pretty good nicknames. We had one offensive guard we called Pancho. I was the Animal. They called the middle linebacker, Jenkins, Baby Face. Our wide receiver was Cookie Thompson. We had a tailback by the name of Wilson, who we called Smooth. Les Goodman, a halfback, was Lightning. He played with the Green Bay Packers. 'Lightning, hey Lightning!' He could fly. Mark Herman, our safety who got drafted by the St. Louis Cardinals, we called him Herm, Big Herms. He had the body of a bodybuilder. Big Herms.

"A lot of the guys hung around together. I was never really friendly with many people because I was always in the weight room. I would never go out socializing. Maybe that was wrong, but I wanted to achieve something then. I wanted to be something more than what I was, and I worked hard. I worked real hard.

"I think people were afraid of me, maybe because I was so big. At one point I had a 22-inch neck, a 52-inch chest. There was no supervised weight program; nobody to help. I just kept lifting more and more; I didn't know any better.

"Nobody ever got drafted from Yankton. Nobody knew what to do. All you knew about pro football was watching big guys play on TV, so I figured I had to be big, I had to be powerful. I just felt powerful and big and quick, though obviously I wasn't as quick as I should have been—when I got to Denver, they took that weight right off me.

"People at Yankton didn't understand, or maybe they just didn't want to understand. People looked at me and said, 'What's wrong with him?' I didn't have any money, so I wore the same pants, the same boots and sweatshirt, a long-sleeve sweatshirt. I never wore a short-sleeve shirt to show off my arms. I didn't think it was necessary; I wasn't doing it to look good on the beach, I was doing it for a *career*. I was doing it to make my life something.

"I started getting big after my junior year, really massive. I would use my arms a lot. I knocked out some people who played in front of me, broke a few face masks, knocked some teeth out."

DAVE DOWNEY

Friends were hard to come by in those days. Alzado was a curio, a freak, but on his second day there he attracted the attention of Dave Downey—a 6-4, former hockey player from Illinois, the assistant equipment man and student sports editor of the school paper. He handed Alzado his first piece of football equipment, watched him work endless hours in the weight room, and after a while he grew to respect this lonely outcast from New York.

"Right before my junior year, the coach said we were getting a new kid by the name of Lyle Alzado and to go ahead and issue Lyle his equipment. But when he came up to get his stuff, all the good stuff was gone. At Yankton College, the starters got some pretty good equipment, but the new guys and the second stringers got pretty lousy stuff. I remember giving him a ripped jock and holey socks and beat-up pads. It was an inauspicious beginning for a future All-Pro. As he progressed through the football program at Yankton, he moved up into some pretty good equipment.

"The first thing I really noticed about Lyle was his desire. Right from the start it was his goal to play in the NFL, and he let you know it. He let everyone know exactly how he felt: that if he was going to be a starter, then he was going to beat some of these veterans out for their jobs. Since he hadn't played a game and he was unproven and untested, he alienated a lot of the other guys. He came across as a braggart who just shot off his mouth—remember, he hadn't yet played a game. So anyway, a lot of the other guys laughed at him and he got into fights. But in spite of everything, he had a lot of desire. And on the field he was very confident in his ability; he was like a young bull. But off the field, he was a loner. I was one of the few people he was friendly with.

"He may have been uncomfortable around the other guys, but he sure seemed at home around food. Seemed like he could never get enough. At dinnertime he'd go back for fourths and fifths when the rest of us would still be on firsts and seconds.

"The kitchen staff would be ready to close up and go home and they'd be yelling out, 'Alzado, aren't you done yet?' Or before they threw out the mashed potatoes, they'd yell, 'Hey, Alzado, we're about to dump the food!' He'd go running up to the counter, yelling, 'Hold on! Not yet, not yet!' And of course, you've heard about the famous pie-eating contest.

"Seventeen chocolate cream pies. Regulation-size pies. There were no knives and forks; he'd just scoop it up with his hands and literally force it down. Then he'd put his face back into the pan, finish it up, and then he'd go on to the next one. There was pie all over the place. Chocolate cream pie all over the floor, the tables; everybody was covered with chocolate cream pie.

"When Lyle wasn't at football practice he could always be found up in the corner of Nash Gymnasium in the weight-lifting area. A lot of guys who'd go over there would spend maybe an hour or two; Lyle would be there for three, four, five, sometimes six hours at a time—and that's no exaggeration.

"He'd work on his legs, work on his neck, work on his arms, work on his upper body. And if you passed by the weight-lifting area when he was there working out, you'd hear him say, 'Hey, I'm going to play in the

National Football League.' He let everybody know that's what his goal was. Nothing was going to keep him from his goal.

"I used to ask myself: what is there to do in a weight room for five hours? It sure bored the hell out of *me*. And sometimes I'd go over and I'd talk to him for a while, but generally he didn't want to be bothered when he was lifting weights.

"He'd do three sets of ten on a particular exercise, then he'd stop and run down to the other end of the gym, run back, loosen up a little bit, and then go through it again. It was amazing. He'd keep going for hours and hours.

"He had a few guys who used to lift with him, but none of them would stay around for the full five hours. Some would come and go, but Lyle would always be there. And again, his dedication turned off a lot of his teammates. Especially when he'd tell people he was going to play in the NFL. They thought he was just shooting off his mouth, that he was just trying to get in good with the coaches.

"It upset the other guys, and they laughed at him: 'Yeah, sure, Alzado. You're going to play in the National Football League. Right. Sure. And the cow's going to fly to the moon, too.'

"And those guys are now selling insurance, teaching in Iowa and Long Island and several places in between, and Lyle's playing in the National Football League. And since Lyle's made it big with the Broncos, I know a lot of guys who thought he was an ass in college think he's a hell of a guy right now... *especially when they need tickets.*

"On top of everything else, Lyle must have seemed like a real freak to some of these guys. He never had any money. His warm-weather wardrobe consisted of a couple of pairs of old blue jeans and a white tee shirt. In the wintertime he had his old Army jacket to wear over the tee shirts. I mean, he literally didn't have clothes to wear. He'd wear either Army boots or tennis shoes. And his dormitory room was always barren. No clothes or rugs, no pictures on the walls, no posters or other assorted paraphernalia. Lyle never had any of that. He had a few weights in his room, and tiger's milk and a bottle of protein pills too. Very few books. He just didn't have the money for extras.

"I live in Denver now, and I see Lyle every now and then, and the most impressive thing is to see him on one of his speaking engagements—talking to a kid's group or something. He's extremely professional, very polished. The first time I ever attended one of his speaking engagements—after he'd made it with the Broncos—I was absolutely amazed, really shocked. He had so much self-confidence, self-assurance; he knew exactly what he was talking about. He had the audience right in the palm of his hand.

"I thought I knew Lyle pretty well, but I was totally amazed at the way he handled himself, the way he presented an anecdote about his past life. He just captivated the audience. Afterward, when he finished, the place was hushed. Then he said, 'Does anybody have any questions?'

"All at once, a hundred hands shot into the air. I was flabbergasted; I was amazed at how far he'd come. I mean, where had he gotten all this?

"I first moved out to Denver in 1972, Lyle's second year with the club. I hadn't seen him for quite a few years, and I didn't know if he'd remember me.

"I don't know why I did it, but I went out to the airport one night to meet the team plane after the Broncos had beaten the 49ers in an exhibition game. There was a pretty good crowd out there, and the players filed off single file. They were all signing autographs, and I was standing in the back, kind of against the wall. You know, after a guy's made it—

after he's become a professional athlete—you think, well, he might treat you differently. He might not recognize you.

"I remember my ex-wife Kerry saying to me, 'David, can I go with you to the plane to meet Lyle?'

"I didn't want to be embarrassed in case he didn't recognize me, or in case he didn't want to be bothered with me anymore. After all, it had been four years. I didn't want to be embarrassed in front of my wife, so I said, 'No, you stay home.'

"So I was standing there as the players were coming off the plane. And Lyle was even with me; he was walking by me. He turned and he looked at me, then looked forward again. But then he looked at me and he started shouting, 'Dave Downey! Dave Downey! Dave Downey!' And he broke out of the line and came running over. He grabbed me and hugged me and pulled over Paul Smith and Pete Duranko and Billy Thompson, introduced them to me, took down my phone number and stuff. That's the kind of person Lyle is. About a week later Kerry and I and Lyle and his girlfriend—who at the time was Sharon Pike—all got together for dinner at our place in Denver. Sharon and Kerry became extremely close friends, and they still are today."

There was one group at Yankton that didn't see Alzado as a freak, as a massive brooding giant who liked to cave in face masks—the kids, particularly the handicapped kids. They saw him as a friend, nothing more or nothing less.

Last year Alzado won the Whizzer White Award as Pro Football's Man of the Year for his work with charitable and community organizations, especially handicapped children's groups. That part of Lyle's life started at Yankton. It started the day he was sitting in the athletic director's office, and the A.D.'s wife asked him to help move some chairs in the gym.

The Fighting Greyhounds of Yankton

• • •

"I went over to the gymnasium and started moving the chairs, and about ten minutes later, 19 or 20 handicapped kids walked in and started playing this game, a kickball kind of game. I was sitting on the side, and this one little girl came over to me and said, 'Will you come play with us?'

"I said, 'I can't play your game.'

"She said, 'It's not *my* game, it's *every*body's game.'

"It laid on me like a bomb. Nobody'd ever said that to me before. I was just learning all these things about people and what they feel. So I changed my major from physical education to special education.

"And the athletic director's wife invited me again. She said, 'Do you want to come over to help us train these kids for the State games?' I said yes, and they made me the coach.

"It changed my life when I started working with those kids, totally changed my life. It gave me an outlook on athletics, on the battle some people have to face, that is very difficult to see and understand unless you are around these athletes. You talk about the great athletes, wide receivers and running backs in the NFL, they can't compare with these people. They're twice as courageous, twice as tough.

"I think some of the violence in me started to disappear. I said to myself, 'Here I am destroying, and here they are creating. What right do I have?' I learned to control it.

"There was one girl who told me she loved me, every day. She was 12, but with the mental capacity of a seven-year-old. One of the first hard experiences I had with kids was to work with this girl. We gave out permission slips to go to the State games at the University of South Dakota, and I kept asking this girl, Sherry, to bring in her permission slip. She wouldn't bring it in. 'Where's your permission slip?' I'd say. 'I want you to participate.' She wouldn't bring it in. One day I caught her mother after school and I said, 'Can you give me the permission slip so Sherry can participate?' You know what she told me? She said, 'I can't worry about Sherry, I've got five other kids to worry about.' The apathy of some parents was incredible. I signed the permission slip myself and almost got thrown out. Her mother got mad. *Real* mad.

"The State games were tremendous. One of our kids was a winner in the broad jump. She had a brace on her leg and she was mentally retarded, but she won the broad jump with this thing on her leg. She ran over to me, and after I put a medal around her she put her arms around me and kissed me. She said, 'I love you, thank you.'

"None of the other guys on the Yankton team, none of the athletes worked with these kids. It bothers me a lot when I know athletes have the ability to do something with kids and don't do it. There are players on the Broncos who work with kids, but I don't know in what depth. It bothers me when I know our guys are in the position they are, but they ignore people who need them. It angers me.

"Anyway, my life changed drastically at that point. I'd play with the kids, throw softballs, run with them, go to class with them, visit with them. And I just kept doing it and doing it, still working out with weights too. And I had to study to stay in school, so I started studying at night like a madman.

"Even with all that, I still wasn't accepted by people in the school. I was accepted by some of the teachers, maybe, but not by many of the students. They didn't see anything more than a football maniac. They didn't know.

"They didn't respect anything about me or what I was doing. I worked very hard; I'd be in the gym till 12 o'clock some nights working out, running, playing basketball, lifting weights, jumping rope.

"One particular rejection, though, hurt me worst of all. I went out with a girl named Shirley Horner. She was a medical technologist at Mount Marty. She taught me about religion and God, taught me how to study. Her parents didn't think I was good enough for her; I might have married her otherwise.

"I found out how her parents felt by reading a letter they'd written her. I was looking through some of her books, one time while she was interning in the Methodist Hospital, and I found the letter. It was opened already, so I decided to read it. It said, 'We love Lyle, but we don't think he's good enough for you.' I always told Shirley I'd give her anything she wanted, but it never turned out that way. She was a very devoted family woman, and she wouldn't go against her parents.

"I was crushed. She was the first woman I ever cared about, and I was never involved with any other woman at Yankton. I liked girls, sure, Shirley was the first woman I ever really got involved with.

"She married a doctor she met in South Dakota. I just got a Christmas card from her."

FOUR:

A Scout's Diary

When I first got together with Stan Jones in the Bronco camp, he told me: "Lyle, if you show you have some potential, if you work hard, you'll be around."

—Lyle

1971 NFL Draft: The Denver Broncos on the fourth round (pick from Boston) select Lyle Alzado, DE, Yankton College, 6-3, 252.

Stan Jones, the defensive line coach—a former Chicago Bear All-Pro at offensive guard and defensive tackle—wanted to pick Alzado higher. "Dammit, we'll lose the guy, we'll lose him!" Jones was complaining in the Broncos' office. "Keep your shirt on," they told him. "He'll still be around."

"Still be around, hell!" Jones said. "A kid like that comes along once in a lifetime."

Jones remembers: "All the coaches had to scout an area in those days, and my area was from Utah all the way across Idaho into Washington. I was on the way back from a scouting trip, heading down to look at Montana State at Bozeman. On the way through a little town near Deer Lodge, I stopped because I had some engine trouble. Skipping gears or something. I was pretty lucky...I pulled into Deer Lodge, Montana—where the State Penitentiary is, in the middle of nowhere—and got to a Chevy garage just before five o'clock on a Friday. I said to myself, boy are *you* in luck. Just got there before they closed. So I went in and said, 'Say, can you fix this thing?' The guy there asked what was the matter. When I told him, he said, 'Jesus, you need a mechanic for that. Nearest one's a distributor, a Chevrolet distributor. We won't have a mechanic in here till Tuesday or Wednesday.' I told him I couldn't wait that long, and he suggested I try to make it into Butte. So I went to Butte, and next morning I went to the mechanic. He said, 'It's gonna take a little while to fix this thing. You got anything to do in town? If you've got some business here I'll take you to where you want to go, then I'll pick you up when you're ready. By that time it should be done.' I said,

'Do you have a school here in town?' He said, 'Yeah, we have Montana Tech, it's up on the hill.' The school looked like something Jim Thorpe might still be going to; you know, it looked like the Carlisle Indian School.

"It was a desolate place, all old buildings. The gym was like an old YMCA, with a track running around and a wooden floor. Some lady was there cleaning the floor of this old gym, and nobody else was around. It was Saturday.

"So I said to the lady waxing the floor, 'Is there a football coach here in this building?'

"She said, 'Yes, he's upstairs. You're in luck.'

"I walked upstairs and there was this guy, typing his brochure all by himself in his little cubbyhole. The whole office, everything included, wasn't much bigger than a closet. I introduced myself, told him I was scouting for the Broncos, and he said, 'My God, who are you looking for?' He was all excited. Anyway, we got out some film of a game they had played against Yankton—the Copper Bowl game in Butte. Montana had a kid by the name of Heeter, a pretty good halfback, and I saw him in the film, but this one defensive end just kept popping up all the time. The Heeter kid wasn't a bad halfback, and he got drafted by somebody, but in the meantime I kept seeing this same defensive kid, No. 80. I said, 'Who is this fellow here?' He said, 'That's Lyle Alzado. Plays at Yankton College.'

"So we got all interested in this kid and homed in on him a little. And, as a result, we drafted him. He was just all over the damn place, making tackles. It just seemed like the same guy kept making them; they just seemed to stick out. The more I looked at this film, the more intrigued I got by this Alzado kid.

"He didn't look like a giant. I was a little surprised he was as big as he was because he looked so damn quick. There was just something about him; he was making something happen. He was always involved in something, he was all over the field, he moved well, he had quickness and showed a lot of things—but then I wasn't too sure of the caliber of people he was playing against. Nevertheless, the movement was there, plus the fact that he was doing something. I've seen a lot of football players who were pretty good, but they weren't as crucial a factor on the game as he was. Phil Olsen comes to mind. Other players may look good and do everything well, but when the game's over you say, 'If he hadn't been there, there wouldn't have been any difference in the game.' Lyle wasn't like that. He was always making things happen.

"After we drafted Lyle, we flew him out and I met him at the airport. He came in to sign his contract. First I picked up his high school coach, Jack Martilotta—his agent at the time—and Jack said, 'You've got to be patient with him. He's a good kid.'

"I said, 'Jack, I know all about him,' and the first thing Lyle said when he got off the plane was, 'Boy, when I saw you and the coach standing there, I could have gone through that wall.' He was all fired up. We took him up to a club—the Mt. Vernon Club, in the Lookout Mountains area, a kind of country club with a golf course, and an eating place with smorgasbord-type food. We went in, and I thought I'd take the coach in and we'd have a cocktail or something. We went into the bar, obviously the bar section, and the restaurant was over on the other side.

"The cocktail waitress came over and said, 'What would you like to have, sir?' and looked at Lyle. And he said, 'Do you have steaks here?' *He ordered steak in the cocktail lounge.* And of course he didn't have a necktie—didn't have one or couldn't get one or whatever. She just stared at him like he was a freak. Then we go over to eat at the smorgasbord. Lyle thought he was in Disneyland. It was like a candy store to him. You could eat anything you want, all this mess, so he had a tremendous time. And then he went out and signed his contract.

"When he came to camp from the All-Star game,

damned if he didn't gain a lot of weight. He got up to about 280 pounds, which was far too heavy for him. Somebody must have told him he ought to gain some weight or something. I didn't know what kind of shape he was in. Lou Saban had told me to take him out early before practice and run him a mile and a half, that was one of the tests we gave.

"I took him out. Nobody was there. But just as I said, 'On your mark, get set, *go!*' and he started off, every damn water sprinkler on that football field came on. It was funny, he was running through those damned water sprinklers, slushing around there for a mile and a half on this measured-off area. I just watched his reaction, to see whether he was going to try to quit. It would have been a good reason to quit, and I was just curious. He ran that whole mile and a half, never quit, and damned if he didn't run a hell of a fast time. I was amazed, at 280 pounds he ran a 12-minute test-type of thing, better than a mile and a half, whatever it was. I was impressed by that. I knew he was strong, I knew he was fast, but I was curious to know what kind of endurance he might have. And guts. He was a tiger that day, and he still is. He plays hard the whole time he's on the football field, every play, as hard as any man who ever played the game."

FIVE:

Making It

You're our rookie. We're gonna take care of you.
— Paul Smith and Rich Jackson

THEY STILL talk about the depth and quality of the 1971 rookie crop: Jim Plunkett and John Riggins, Mike Adamle, Ken Anderson, Jim Braxton, Harold Carmichael, Bob Chandler and Clarence Davis, Tony Greene, Mel Gray, Dan Pastorini, Jack Tatum, Marv Montgomery, Jack Ham and John Brockington.

No less impressive was the crop of defensive linemen, and Lyle Alzado of little Yankton College was lost in the shuffle. Only the top draft choices were picked for the All-Star game in Chicago, and Alzado was an afterthought. He was a late pick.

"I never thought I'd play in the college All-Star game. I didn't make any big All-Americas, being from a little place like Yankton. And I was sitting at home, the summer previous to the All-Star camp, and I told Mark Lyons that if they called me I'd hang up on them. I wouldn't play in any damn All-Star game. Then they called me up and said, 'Lyle, we'd like you to be at the All-Star camp,' and I said, 'Yeah, all right, great ...WOW!" I told them I'd pay my own way down, and they let me. I hopped in the car next day and drove out there.

"Nobody knew me. It was an awesome training camp. I mean we had *athletes*, guys who had played tremendous football during their whole career. Blanton Collier was the coach, and obviously he played the people who were first-team All-Americans and so on. The defensive ends were Richard Youngblood, Richard Harris, Bob Bell, Wilbur Young, and myself. Wilbur and I were backups. I played a quarter, a quarter and a half. We played the Baltimore Colts, and I played against a guy named Sullivan—Dan Sullivan, No. 71.

"I went in there and banged heads and butted and slapped and punched. I didn't get much accomplished. I learned; it was a fabulous learning experience.

Sullivan smiled a lot. He's a good guy. He laughed and smiled, kidded with me and said, 'Okay, rookie,' and all that kind of stuff. But that's the way it was, an initiation.

"He position-blocked me, grabbing and turning. He used his hands on me, and I wasn't used to that. It was a good experience for me. I didn't know much about so many things. Anyway, they only beat us 24-17.

"The first chance I got was against the Chicago Bears, in the last exhibition game of '71. The week before that, Pete Duranko—the starting right defensive end—had gone down with a knee injury. But there was Marty Amsler, a fourth-term veteran, in front of me. And I came from the All-Star camp. Even worse, I was late. But Stan Jones said, 'Lyle, this is your shot. You're going to start against Chicago next week. You show me that you've got the guts, that you can play, and everthing's going to be all right.'

"I went in there and made seven or eight tackles and had a quarterback sack. I was playing against a tackle named Jackson—not Noah, a different tackle by the name of Jackson—and I came out and had to have three or four stitches put in my nose. Next week Stan told me I made the squad. I felt like picking up the phone and calling everyone in the world and telling them I made it. It was tremendous; it was my chance. Stan said, 'You've got your chance. This is it for you.' He could have started with the other guy. That next week, when they cut the veteran, Marty Amsler, Stan said, 'I believe in you, and I'm going to work with you and help you.' And he did—he sure as hell did."

The Broncos were getting ready for Lou Saban's fifth and last year as head coach. They had been the joke of the AFC's Western Division, an almost perennial last-place finisher. In 1970 they had started the season with three straight victories; they had hung onto the division lead for almost half a season, and then they had collapsed with six losses in their last eight games.

Making It

The offense was in a state of flux, with Steve Ramsey and Don Horn battling for the starting quarterback job, but the defense, led by All-Pro left end Richie Jackson, was a unit filled with pride. Fifteen defensive club records had been set the previous year. And the Broncos had allowed only seven touchdowns rushing. The Bronco fans had been loyal—and patient. All seven 1970 home games had been sellouts.

Rookies were not subjected to the usual hazing that is a matter of course in most pro camps. At Denver they were welcomed. Any help appreciated.

"Here's something great about the Bronco camp, and it's one reason why I'll always be indebted to two guys—Paul Smith and Richie Jackson, defensive left tackle, defensive left end. You know how terrible camp can be for a rookie, how nervous and alone and scared you are? Well, I wasn't nervous when I went to camp, because the minute I walked into camp I went through the food line and sat down where all the veterans were—Lou Saban and all those guys. Paul Smith and Rich Jackson came and sat in the two seats next to me and put their arm around me and they said, 'You're our rookie. We're gonna take care of you.' Can you imagine? Two superstars, All-Star pros, taking care of a rookie like that! They took me riding up and down Colfax Avenue for ice cream on their days off, and they'd take me out to the lake. They just took care of me from the start.

"Sure, they hazed me a little. They'd call my room around twelve at night, forty-five minutes or an hour after curfew, and Smitty would say, 'Lyle, Rich wants to talk to you.'

"Rich would say, 'Lyle, I want you to go out and get me two hamburgers, two orders of French fries, and two large Cokes.' And to get out of the Continental Denver Hotel you had to go by the coach's office. So I'd sneak underneath the coach's office, Lou Saban's office, at about 12:30 at night, and get the hamburgers, then sneak back in, give them to Rich and Paul, and sneak back to my room. This happened every night.

"But they took care of me, too, and taught me things in training camp. Take it easy, relax, they said. They would take me aside and show me techniques, and it was harder because I was even moodier then than I am now. And it was difficult to relate to me because I was so intense. That's just the way I am. They like me for what I am, and I appreciated that then as much as I do now.

"Rich and Smitty showed me a move they invented, called the halo spinner, a pass-rush technique. You rush upfield seven yards, dip your shoulder, throw your right arm around, and you spin back underneath. It could break a guy's hold on your jersey—a devastating move, especially if it's done right. If it's done right, you can't beat it; there's no way to block it. It depends on what side you're playing. If you play the left side, you dip your right shoulder; if you're playing the right side, you dip your left shoulder.

"They taught me the head butt, grab, and pull. You aim right for the guy's face mask. But things would come hard because it took me time to learn that stuff.

"So out on the field I'd be working on all these moves, and then I'd go to the dining room at night and have to sing my school song, the Yankton song. I'll give you ten bucks if you can sing one line, if anyone can. Listen to this:

Hail Yankton College,
Center of the Universe and Continent.
We're the Black and the Gold, fight! fight! fight!
Fight for the Black and Gold...

Pretty good, huh? I made up most of it, but the guys in the dining room didn't know that. They'd laugh and throw rolls and tell me to sit down.

"I'll always feel close to Paul Smith and Rich

Making It

Jackson because of the way they treated me when I was a rookie. Smitty's my roommate now, has been almost since the beginning. Nobody else treated me like those two guys did. Take a guy like Duranko... Pete's one of the finest people I've met in pro football, but he was very nervous because they needed an aggressive pass-rusher and drafted me to fill the gap.

"As a matter of fact, a year ago I met a friend of Pete's who said, 'You know, Lyle, when Pete Duranko got hurt, he came to see me and said, "You see that kid play? I'll never get my spot back again."' And I thought, that's the greatest compliment ever paid to me by anybody.

"Rookies weren't mistreated on the Broncos because Lou Saban wouldn't allow it. Lou Saban demanded that you help out because Denver was in a state of shock. Before that, though, they were kind of rough on rookies. But by the time I got to Denver, there was a loser atmosphere around the club with most guys.

"Only problem was, they didn't know how to win. Lou was a winner. Stan Jones was a winner. But most of the other guys were losers. I could just feel it. I could feel it when we took the field. We knew we'd lose, some way or other we would lose the game. You could feel it in the locker room before the game. The intense feeling of the defense was there, but we always figured something would happen and we'd lose. And we were usually right.

"We went to Philadelphia and we were beating the hell out of them all day. Three minutes left in the fourth quarter, they blocked a punt and scored a touchdown and we got beat 17-15. Miami game, the half-a-loaf game, we're ahead, 10-3, a few minutes left in the fourth quarter: Warfield goes on a down and out, they throw him a ball, touchdown. We had an opportunity to win the game and we wouldn't throw a pass deep in our own territory and take a chance of losing the game.

Held onto the ball, game ended in a 10-10 tie. Lou made the statement, 'Half a loaf is better than none.' Next time we took the field, the fans threw half-loaves of bread at us.

"There was selfishness—which happens on every team—and jealousy. A guy makes All-Pro and the guy says, 'Well, I should have made it long before so-and-so did.' Guys would jump up in the locker room and yell and scream—threaten each other.

"It devastated me. I was on a losing team for the first time in my life, and I couldn't stand it. It drove me crazy. But I kept quiet because I wasn't the greatest defensive player in the world, either.

"Rich and Paul told me, 'Lyle, keep your mouth shut. Do what you're supposed to do and you'll be all right.' So I did.

"There were two black guys taking care of me, but it didn't matter whether they were black, white, green, or purple because—where I grew up—people were people. I didn't look at it as black and white; I never looked at it that way. And then, when Paul Smith and I roomed together after Rich Jackson left the Broncos my second year, I still didn't think about it. Paul Smith was my friend Paul Smith—not Paul Smith, a black man."

SIX:
A Girl from Yankton

I mean, there he was: 285 pounds, wearing a maroon tweed leisure suit with maroon leather strips all the way down the sleeves and pants, a great big wide-open collar unbuttoned nearly down to the waist, jewelry hanging all over him. He comes in, leans on the bar and asks for some exotic drink, then he asks me for a dance....
—Sharon Alzado

AFTER HIS rookie season with the Broncos, Lyle Alzado came back to Yankton to finish the five credits in English lit and physiology he still needed for his degree. He was already a celebrity. Yankton players simply didn't make it in the NFL, and people who had ignored him when he was in college were now coming around to chat about the Broncos' chances in 1972, and life in pro football.

When he arrived, Lyle found a room in the Yankton gym had been named after him, the Lyle Alzado Weight Room.

"The reason they did it," says his wife, Sharon, "is that they didn't have a real weight room, and Lyle had used part of his Bronco check to buy weights for them."

Sharon Alzado—Sharon Pike, as she was then—had never met Lyle when he was a full-time student at Yankton, even though she was born and bred in Yankton and he had been one of the town's main attractions. She was at school 30 miles away, the University of South Dakota, when he was at Yankton.

"Even at South Dakota U, everyone knew of Lyle Alzado," she says.

Her father had taken her to see Yankton play. He had been something of a Yankton legend himself. Lean and rugged at 6-3, 190, Bill Pike had played offensive and defensive end on the Yankton football team just after World War II. In track and field his exploits were even more formidable.

One year Pike, his coach, and three teammates piled into a car and drove to Wisconsin to compete in the Beloit Relays. They took fourth place and Pike scored 26 points himself, finishing first in the high and low hurdles, the high jump, and the discus, and placing in the shot put, javelin, and mile relay.

One of the largest liquor distributors in South Dakota and the owner of a local credit company, Pike had been a supporter of Yankton athletics through the years. He kept track of its successes, worked out in the gym—and took a special interest in the big defensive end from New York.

Sharon remembers: "I've been an avid football fan all my life, and athletically inclined, and I came home from college one weekend to go to a Yankton College game with my dad. This was Lyle's junior year, and I was a freshman in college. My dad handed me his binoculars and said, 'You've got to watch his kid Alzado. He's great.' Yankton beat some college 72-0 that day because Lyle just ran wild through the whole offensive line; kept sacking the quarterback. That was the first time I saw Lyle, watching him raising hell through my binoculars.

"He didn't have any technique, no finesse; he just overpowered the two or three guys who tried to block him. That's all he did: he just overpowered them with brute strength.

"I had played paddle ball games in college during the noon hours while Lyle was going to school," Bill Pike says, "and I knew who he was. I'd seen him around, but I didn't make any effort to get to know him personally or anything. I'd just speak to him when he came in from the weight room or something like that. He knew my name, but that was about all. I don't think he knew Sharon was my daughter.

"My wife and I supported the Quarterback for the Century Club, where we donated money for the Yankton College athletics. We went to all the games, every game, and knew all the players personally, you might say, because you'd see them downtown or at school. To us, Lyle was just another Eastern kid. Yankton used to get a lot of them in those days, before our two good recruiters left and the program dropped way down. I always kidded him about his combat boots. You know, something like, 'Say, you need a pair of shoes, fella?' Because he always had combat boots on. But basically I thought of him as just another

Eastern football recruit who'd come and go; we'd never see him again.

"We used to have the players downtown, and we had lots of things for them, trying to promote goodwill with the merchants and helping the people get to know all the players, and we really liked them all because we knew they were good football players. We had quarterbacks and receivers and defensive men like this for a period of maybe ten years when we were getting guys from the East, when Yankton reached an all-time high of 650 students. And we had good teams; we were really tough. Then we lost the two recruiters. And Yankton College has never taken advantage of Lyle being in pro football. Their program is just going downhill.

"Anyway, toward the end of Lyle's career at Yankton, he really dominated in football. He was across the line so quick that the offensive tackle just couldn't even touch him. He either knocked down an interference man and had the runner, or else he had the quarterback. Time after time, you just couldn't believe it.

"We had people who didn't care about football, but they would come to games just to watch Lyle. But he would pick up the other quarterback, help him up, which the crowd really didn't want to see. They wanted to see him stomp the guy and things like that. It was in that era before you started helping your opponent up. That came about right after his time in college ball.

"When my daughter first met Lyle, my wife and I were still in Phoenix, and Sharon called one night and said, 'I've got a date with Lyle Alzado.' I can't recall what I first said, but I think I told her make sure there was somebody else in the house. We didn't have any fear about our girls—Sharon or her sister, Jane—because we always told them, 'If you can't come home and tell us about it you shouldn't be doing it.' And it worked out fine."

After her sophomore year, Sharon Pike dropped out of the University of South Dakota and got a job in Yankton. Lyle Alzado was just a name she heard around town, around the dinner table, an exotic import who had played out the string at Yankton and was now on his way back to the big time.

Sharon remembers: "Lyle was drafted by Denver, and naturally we were all claiming we knew him. After his rookie year, he needed five more hours to graduate, and he came back to school. I had just quit school, after the end of the semester; I was trying to decide on a major.

"I was staying alone in the house, and one night my girlfriend called me up to go to a Yankton High School basketball game. So we decided to go. And then afterward we went to a place called Jim's Tap, which I had probably only been in like two or three times. It was kind of a Yankton hangout. But that night we went there and we were having a good time.

"And all of a sudden, about 11 o'clock in walked Lyle Alzado, big rookie star of the Denver Broncos wearing a maroon tweed leisure suit, with maroon leather strips all the way down the sides of the sleeves and all the way down the pants, with this great big wide-open collar unbuttoned to nearly the waist, jewelry hanging all over him. He comes in, leans on the bar and asks for some exotic drink, then he asks me for a dance. The dance floor—this place called Jim's Tap probably has the smallest bar in Yankton—has to be like ten by ten, and with Lyle out there dancing it was even smaller. He's always been a fantastic dancer—he grew up in New York and I think he was a born dancer anyway—and he was taking up the whole floor with all his moves.

"Then, after the dance, he said in this soft voice—this big brute with such a soft manner—he said, 'Hello,

I'm Lyle Alzado.' I thought, he introduced himself to me? I mean everybody in the world know's he's Lyle Alzado and he followed me and introduced himself to me? He said, 'Well I haven't seen you here before.' You know, the typical line. And I said, 'I haven't been in here before.' Really scintillating repartee.

"So we sat and talked. He said he'd follow me home in his car. It was a February evening; it was cold and snowing out, and he wanted to make sure I got home okay.

"So we got out and started to walk to the car. He was driving an Eldorado, custom-made; he had his name engraved on the dashboard, and this was only after his rookie year. He came from poverty to—what do they pay rookies, $12,000 a year? He thought he was a millionaire. I couldn't believe this guy. So he followed me home in my little Camaro.

"I grew up quite naive. When you grow up in South Dakota you don't really know what's going on, and I thought he was just being a gentleman. So he followed me home, then came in and asked for a baloney sandwich. He said, 'I'm really hungry.'

"I said, *'A baloney sandwich?'* He had baloney and mayonnaise and bread, nothing else. I thought, my parents aren't going to believe Lyle Alzado is here, sitting in our home having a baloney sandwich.

"He ate the sandwich, then went and sat down in our family room and started flipping through the paper and everything. That was at two o'clock in the morning. He just kept sitting there, and I thought, Are you *ever* going to leave?

"A little bit later I said, 'Well, I'm really getting tired.' He always tells everybody that I threw him out of our house. I don't remember actually throwing him out, but I did ask him to leave. Finally he left, but I guess he couldn't believe I didn't invite him to spend the night at my house when I was all alone.

"He called me the next day and said, 'Let's go to a movie.' There are two movie theaters in Yankton, and he wanted to see *Airport*. He'd never seen *Airport*. Unbelievable! I'd seen it three times, but I said, 'Fine, I'll go.' I sat through *Airport* for the fourth time on my first real-live date with him. And from that moment on we saw each other all the time.

"The first time I ever watched Lyle work out I was horrified because of the grotesque faces he made, and the terrible sounds—the grunts and groans. I looked at him and thought, is this what working out is? *Total* perspiration. I thought, is this what I admired so much?

"But I finally realized he was very dedicated. When I met Lyle he weighed 285, and right now he's at 245. I thought he was so massive—like a giant balloon. I couldn't tell him to his face that he was fat; he thought it was all muscle. And he didn't have a beard then; he had puffy cheeks instead. But his belly was where he had most of his weight."

For the conservative Bill and Edith Pike, who had lived in Yankton all their lives, the addition of Lyle Alzado to the household was interesting—but it took some getting used to.

Bill Pike remembers: "I didn't dislike the idea that Sharon was going with Lyle, but I can't say I really liked it. He was quite a bit bigger then—he was 20 pounds heavier—and he was really naive and crude and all those things rolled into one. Embarrassing. I never saw a person change so rapidly, once he got recognized in pro football. What he says to those handicapped kids comes right from his heart; he doesn't force himself to make up a speech and go talk to them. He can talk about football or things that interest handicapped kids, and he can really talk to them.

"Lyle says he never had a real father image, and the

A Girl from Yankton

first time he heard from his dad in the last fifteen years or so was when he made All-Pro and his dad called him. I guess his father just actually up and left him and that was it. He didn't care what the hell happened. We created kind of a warm atmosphere for him at our house. We tried to, anyway, to make him feel like he was one of us, and it didn't make any difference if he was a football player or anything else."

The only serious relationship Lyle Alzado ever had with a woman was with Shirley Horner, and it had left its scars. He had first seen Sharon as a cute chick in a college hangout, nothing more.

"Green and red ski sweater," he says. "Blond hair in pigtails. A lovely little coed. I guess I had ideas of staying over at her house that night—more because I expected it than anything else—but underneath, maybe I was hoping she wouldn't let me.

"I wanted to be around her all the time. She was fresh and honest, and her parents were very decent to me—very decent—after they got over their initial surprise.

"I guess I was thinking about marriage pretty soon after I met her, but I didn't know how to go about it. Marriage! That's quite a step. So I did the next best thing: I asked her to come out to Denver to live, so I could keep seeing her. I'm not really sure what I wanted from this girl, I only knew I had to hold onto her.

"I knew she was the best thing that ever happened to me in my life. I mean *the absolute best*."

Sharon remembers: "I wanted to be in Denver because I was so fascinated by this guy. I'm sure when he was in Denver he had all the women he ever wanted, and I'm sure that's what he expected of me, but maybe that's what attracted him to me—I wasn't like those others. You know, even when I went to college I'd never had a drink. Maybe a sip of Dad's beer, that's all.

"And my high school years were the best of my life. I

grew up having 'most everything I wanted, having a very loving family, very close, and we would do everything together. That's the way I grew up: not really wealthy, but being where I had everything I really wanted. But Lyle grew up not having anything he wanted, not much love, nobody who really cared. He's had nothing but a totally oppressive background—totally opposite from me.

"It was hard for me to understand some things, like when he said he'd been in jail. If we had met when we were both in high school, I'd have thought he was the most tremendous hood I'd ever met. I wouldn't have even looked at him a second time.

"Lyle proposed to me pretty soon after we met, but we didn't get married until May of '75, two and a half years later. When he proposed to me I wasn't ready to marry him; I hardly knew him and I wasn't ready for this kind of thing, professional athlete and all. I'm sure I offended him totally because he's so sensitive. I was completely shocked when he asked me. But I think he just saw the look on my face and knew I wasn't really ready for marriage. He didn't bring it up again for a long time.

"To be honest, marriage was the farthest thing from my mind at the time. I thought to myself, I really like Lyle, and this would be fun—move to Denver, date a professional football player—but it was a fantasy with me. And I never really believed I would fall in love with him. Luckily he had the patience to wait it out. Then, by the time I was ready to marry him, he decided *he* wasn't ready to get married. So that's why our relationship went around and around for such a long time. I finally ended up moving to Florida for several months because Lyle was postponing our marriage. Maybe the absence did it, because we got married soon after that. I think we needed that separation.

"I've never met his father. When I first met his mother, we were just going together, and I went to New

A Girl from Yankton

York to meet her. Lyle kept preparing me for the place, kept saying, 'Now remember, don't expect too much.'

"But I really didn't expect it to be as bad as it was. She lived in a building that should have been condemned. Plaster was falling off the walls. It was in a terrible neighborhood, and there were roaches all over the place.

"It was a small two-bedroom apartment. It was his mother, two sisters, his brother, and Lyle and me—plus his sister had a friend. I slept with his sister in a bunk bed. It was really unbelievable. The neighborhood was falling apart. In fact, right before I got there, a fire broke out in an apartment on the next floor. Faulty wiring. It destroyed practically the whole floor of that building. The place was really awful, and it was so dirty!

"I met his grandparents when we went to dinner at their house. They cooked all this Jewish food, and it was really hard for me to get it down. I just never did acquire a taste for Jewish foods. But I sat there, trying to get it down, trying to please his grandparents. They were very nice to me.

"I'd never tried anything like that. The matzoh-ball soup just stuck in my throat. I couldn't handle the food. Everybody else was eating it, so I thought it couldn't be *that* bad. I figured it must be just that I'd never tasted it before. And there I was, trying so hard to eat it there were tears in my eyes. There is only one Jewish family in Yankton, so it's all very foreign to me.

"But I knew his grandmother liked me because she called me *'shane madele'*, which means 'pretty girl.' Right away I thought, Oh my gosh, what is *that*? But Lyle looked at me, winked, and said, 'That's nice. She likes you.'

"His grandmother died right after we got married. Wonderful people, his grandparents."

SEVEN:

Tombstone

Richie Jackson came up to me one day and said, "Coach, what do I have to do to make All-Pro defensive end?" And since we were going on the road to play the Jets that weekend, I said, "Well, you'd better look good against Joe Namath in New York. That's where you'll get all the publicity."

I don't know whether you recall the kind of game he had in New York that day, but we beat the Jets, 33-24. He was making tackles all over the field, but I recall one particular pass-rush he had on Namath. He beat the man in front of him—Sherm Plunkett, 330 pounds—ran right over the back they had in there to help block him, ran into the goalpost, bounced off, and got Namath. It was the damnedest thing I'd ever seen. All the coaches would sit around looking at films of that play, and we'd start laughing.

His nickname was Tombstone, and he won't be considered one of the all-time greats because his career wasn't long enough, but ask the guys he played against and they'll tell you he was the best.

Lyle Alzado is in that same mold. It's too bad Richie got hurt when Lyle was just starting out, and that their careers didn't overlap more than one year, because if you put them at the defensive ends they'd be like a pair of bookends. You just wouldn't have to worry about stopping the run for a while.

—Stan Jones, defensive line coach, Denver Broncos

HE HAD been a nondescript linebacker for the Oakland Raiders, and he'd played some tight end. The Broncos got him as a throw-in in a five-player trade in 1967. Stan Jones looked him over when he arrived that summer.

"You seem a little big for a linebacker," Jones told him. "I think we'll try you at defensive end."

Jackson stared at him. He had fought his way through the minor leagues; he had been bounced around in the pros. He was 26—old for a second-year player—and he had driven all night, across the mountains, to get to the Broncos' camp.

"Mister," he said. "I'm gonna play somewhere. I've driven as far as I'm gonna drive. Here's where I make my stand."

Richie "Tombstone" Jackson became an All-Pro, and he had a profound effect on Alzado when the two players met four years later. He helped develop the rookie's techniques, and his sad departure from the game a year later taught Alzado one of the harder facts about NFL life: You have to take care of yourself.

"Tombstone and Paul Smith were the guys who took care of me in camp. Let me tell you something Rich Jackson once did for me on the field. It was against Francis Peay, when we were playing Green Bay.

"Peay was Hollywooding me. You know what that means? Talking, acting cocky, grabbing me, shoving me, that kind of thing. I didn't know how to handle it because I didn't have any techniques yet. He was saying, 'You ain't shit. Come on sucker, let's see what you've got,' stuff like that. And I was trying to punch him in the head. I came back in the huddle and Rich Jackson said, 'What's wrong, Lyle?' I said, 'I don't know, this guy's talking to me.' He said, 'He's

Hollywooding you?' You know what he did? Rich switched places with me and knocked the guy out. Head slap. All I heard was *pow*! and this guy was on the floor.

"Then Rich said, 'Here, Lyle. He's all yours.'

"I would watch him on film all the time. I tried to copy him completely, and it hurt me that I couldn't be what Rich was. Rich was too powerful. I never met another man that strong in my life.

"One summer after my rookie year, I wrote Richie Mollo a letter and said I was lifting weights and had bench-pressed 510 pounds. Jackson must have heard about the letter, because the next time I came in the locker room he said, 'Lyle, you bench-pressed 500 pounds, huh?' I said 'Yeah, Rich.' He laughed and put 485 pounds on the bar. I struggled and got it, but I had to struggle with it. Rich added 50 more pounds and benched it easy, smiled, winked at me, and walked out. A true story. Ask Paul Smith.

"Rich played at 245 pounds, 250 the most. I can close my eyes and remember the great games he had. Rich Jackson against Oakland. They built it up all week that Bob Brown—the Boomer—was going to beat Rich Jackson and what a match-up it was going to be and this and that, and they made it sound like Rich was in for big trouble.

"Rich just devastated the poor guy, and the Boomer could hit, believe me—I took some lumps from him. Rich had his nose bleeding, knocked out his teeth, broke his helmet. That's why they outlawed the multiple head slap in those days, exactly why they changed the rule, and later they outlawed it completely.

"I saw Rich knock guys to their knees with the head slap, knock them on their backs. I remember the way he head-slapped Nicolson of Kansas City, head-slapped him from the inside, actually, from his right. He played the left side, and he knocked Nicolson off his feet and onto his side. Then he went into Len Dawson and knocked Dawson's helmet off.

"I tried to copy Rich's head slap, but I couldn't get it going like he did because he was so much stronger than me. I would knock people to their knees once in a while, but Rich could do it anytime he wanted to.

"Bill Hayhoe of the Packers kept holding Rich one game. Rich knocked him to his knees and split his helmet wide open. BAM! Remember that famous picture of Y. A. Tittle on his knees, blood dripping down from his nose? That was Hayhoe. They took him out of the game. Had to.

"You ask people around the league what Rich used to do. Devastating. I admire Paul Smith as a football player, but Rich was the most impressive defensive lineman I've ever seen play. For two or three years he may have been the greatest ever.

"It ended for Rich in '72. He got his knee operated on after seven games in the '71 season, my rookie season. He had a tumor in his knee, and when they operated they found bone deterioration. And he'd been playing on it.

"When he came back in the '72 season, John Ralston had taken over as head coach. I guess Ralston wanted to find out who could play and who couldn't, and they made Rich scrimmage all during camp on that postoperative knee. And that ended Rich's career.

"He was out there hitting in pads when he should have been resting and taking it easy. I never realized Rich had a bad knee while he was playing. All I knew was the next thing, during the night—about the eighth game of the 1971 season—they put him in the hospital and operated. I was at the Quarterback Club, a fans' thing, with Stan Jones, and he got up there and people asked him about Rich. He started talking and said, 'I've never seen Rich on his back before,' and 'Rich isn't the kind of person to lie on his back. I *know* Rich. If he could he'd be here right now...' And Stan started crying. He tried to say more, but he couldn't. He had to sit down. Stan said to me later, 'I love Rich Jackson. These guys are like my sons all over again.'

"Next year Stan went to Buffalo with Lou Saban, and Ralston took over. The veterans would watch Rich trying to scrimmage, and they'd say, 'They're going to ruin Rich's career.'

"When his career ended they traded him to Cleveland. I was stunned and shocked and disappointed. I've never forgiven John Ralston for that. Maybe, down deep, it was one of the reasons I led the Dirty Dozen against Ralston last year, why I wanted him out. It was wrong for him to do that; it was wrong for him to make Rich scrimmage like that. He should have rested Rich. But Ralston had brought in a whole new coaching staff. New trainer, new doctor, new everything and no one on that staff opened his mouth.

"Rich wasn't a complainer. Someone should have said something. Rich played with so much pain at one time, it was incredible. But even in pain he was devastating. I'd go up to his room, and his leg would be propped up on two pillows, swollen up like a balloon. People asked me if I thought about quitting the game after seeing something like that. I didn't. I didn't, because in the streets you learn to survive. That's what I was doing, surviving.

"Rich walked over to me when he found out he was traded to Cleveland. He walked over and shook my hand and said, 'Well, I'm on my way to Cleveland.' I thought he was kidding. I said, 'Come on, will you?' and started walking away. But then when I realized it was true, I turned around with tears in my eyes. All I could say was, 'Thanks, Rich.' He could hardly walk. And his knee is still bad.

"Paul Smith moved to left end, and he became the new Rich Jackson. But three years ago Paul went down with an Achilles tendon. A guy on the Chiefs fell on top of his leg. I could hear the pop all the way across the line.

"He went 'Oh!' and then walked off the field. He wouldn't let anybody carry him off. He walked off the field himself.

"When he came back he had lost that little extra quickness. They moved him around a little bit; played right end, you know, and then they moved him around a little bit more. He's still good now, but not like he used to be.

"One day, right after Paul got hurt, Coach Ralston came over to me and said, 'Lyle, I want you to take over. It's up to you now.' So I did. I played harder, worked harder. Life goes on, you know?"

EIGHT:

The NFL Way

Alzado uses his hands a lot and has a great left hook. If you spit in his beard, he gets so mad he'll fight his man and forget the game. He goes against Ralph Neely of the Cowboys, and should have a good game. Neely is not the spitting type.

—George Young, Miami Dolphins' Director of Pro Scouting, analyzing the Broncos before Super Bowl XII

When you've been a street fighter, sometimes you'll resort to old tactics when you get frustrated. On the field, Art Shell—the Raiders' 295-pound left tackle—is one of the meanest, vilest guys I ever played against. He'll cuss me, grab me, spit in my face, and I'll punch him, spit in his face, and cuss him right back. I might say something about his mother and father, too, but I don't hate the guy, I respect him. People always ask me what it's like to play against Art Shell, but the only way I can describe it is to ask them: "Have you ever been attacked by wild dogs?"

—Lyle Alzado, before the AFC Championship game against the Oakland Raiders.

IT'S AN image Lyle Alzado likes to keep alive, the street fighter in pads and cleats. And during his first few years in the pros, that's what kept him around—his aggressiveness. But when Paul Smith went down, Alzado realized the passing of the guard had reached him, and he was now the veteran defensive lineman and the leader of the unit.

He realized that you don't make All-Pro on your KO record; you make it with moves and quickness and experience. You make it by going out on every play.

When he came into the league he was a pass-rusher. They made the big money; quarterback sacks were fun. Playing the run was difficult. You had to learn to read and adjust and fight the pressure. Defensive ends who knew how to play the run stayed around a long time, but they seldom made the All-Star teams.

"Defensive linemen get recognized by scouts and the media for their pass-rush," says Mike Haffner, Alzado's early teammate on the Broncos and now a TV sportscaster in Denver.

"With so many people up on the line in college to stop the running game, you get lots of help on your pass-rush. And anyway, it's more spectacular for everybody to talk about a player making five sacks against a team.

"But now, with the importance of the running game in professional football, the linemen are forced to learn how to play the run. A defensive lineman needs five years to learn a style that is successful. You have to learn how to play the run on a consistent basis, especially with pursuit. Defensive linemen in college, especially interior linemen, aren't used to that kind of pursuit; they're not used to the kind of speed that an offensive guard has in the National Football League.

"So Lyle had to learn the tricks. He had to learn how to be smart, and he became one of the best defensive ends in the NFL at playing the run—without sacrificing his pass-rush."

Lyle admits that he was unsophisticated in the beginning. "I just ran after the ball and ran upfield, that kind of thing. I had to develop technique, and I developed more concentration: step right, hit right, move to the ball. Gradually, every time I hit, soon as I would make contact with the tackle and do my job, I'd go to the ball, fly to the ball. I didn't care where it was; even if it was on the other side I would go after the ball. I've caught receivers downfield, catching the ball.

"And that's the way I've developed control. As soon as you make contact you do what you're supposed to do and go after the ball. The head slap, which Richie Jackson taught me, was my No. 1 weapon, but this year they outlawed it. So I developed the head-butt technique. Keeps a guy off balance.

"I still have trouble with my pass-rush. There was one night after practice—we'd had pass-rush that day. We had two periods of pass-rush, and I had done something wrong with what they called the shoulder block, and Stan stayed out there with me and helped me. And the year after that I hit 13 quarterbacks.

"You come up real low, you stay low, and as you come to the corner—which is a five-yard corner—you'll turn your shoulder down and come across. You get underneath your man's shoulder and arm, and lift it. Terry Owens was one of the hardest guys I've ever played; 6-8, 300 pounds, massive. But that worked on him. And it worked some on Jim Tyrer.

"A guy who's short and gets off the ball quickly, like Jon Kolb of the Steelers—guys like that I have trouble with. I feel more comfortable with tall guys like Neely. I like to get underneath their shoulder pads and use my strength.

"No one technique works on a guy like Art Shell. In the second game in Denver, I was in on a lot of tackles. That was the most physical game I've had against him.

The NFL Way

I had one play with my forehead! And I remember old head-bumper... My arms were just scrape marks, black-and-blue marks all over the place.

"What makes me annoyed is that when I play against Art Shell, everybody says Art is one of the best. But not *the* best. But every time I play against him I've handled him, and people say, 'Well, they ran outside in the second game.'

"I'm handling the inside hole there against Art Shell, so it's not *my* responsibility to catch the bounce-out 14 yards over there. Still everybody said, 'Well, they were successful because they ran at Alzado,' and this and that.

"A lot of the Cowboys are very cocky. Ralph Neely isn't that way. Ralph is a good, veteran, hard-nosed football player. He does things well. A lot of people think he holds too much, which is just bullshit. He hardly held me the first time I played him. I didn't have that good a pass-rush stay against him. Played the run well, played the pass fair, and that was it.

"You're just not going to dominate a tackle like Ralph all game. He's too good a football player. But there are tackles you *can* dominate. Your offensive linemen can dominate defensive linemen. It just depends on the day.

"Ralph is a good, steady tackle. The offense is very technical. The position block, the backs are very quick, they cut off their blocks very well, Staubach makes the whole thing go forward, and he's very difficult to handle. However, I think defensively we have got too much strength and too much speed for them, and we're too physical. And I think that's how we're going to beat them.

"A really tremendous football player I've played against is Norm Evans. I'll never forget him because I was so excited for this game. I built up for it; I worked hard, hard, hard, and I thought he was one of the better tackles I played against in my rookie year. He was a technician, he was smart, and he didn't hold much. Stayed under control all the time.

"I played against a guy from Kansas City, a big guy named Jim Tyrer who used to sometimes take me to the end and I'd try to punch him. And don't forget Bob Brown, the Boomer. Devastating hitter—oh, was he strong! He was like a sledgehammer. He hit me once and I thought my arm broke. Tremendous power.

"One of the toughest tackles I've played against is Doug Dieken from Cleveland. That guy's tough, down in dirt. He's one of the better ones. I had to do quite a bit of yelling against him.

"Sometimes yelling destroys players' concentration; they get mad. I remember yelling at Dieken, and I spit at Dieken and said, 'You dirty bastard, get your hands off me! Stop holding me!' Bob Adams, the guard next to him, looked around and said, 'Will you two shut up and play football?' But it hurt him to listen to that.

"In our system, a three-man line, we have to play the run first, and I pride myself on the way I play the run. A guy like Harvey Martin... He made All-Pro, but I don't think he plays a run at all. He's a pretty good pass-rusher, and I think he's good, but I think Claude Humphrey is one of the best ends in football because he plays a run and a pass.

"I used to study films of Rich Jackson all the time, to learn to play the run. That Tombstone was devastating. I only studied films of him. Nobody else, just Rich. He could do all phases of the game, and that's rare. A lot of guys in this league right now just play the pass, or they just play the run; it can't be both. A few people can. Jerry Sherk plays the run and plays the pass. I watch him on film. I think Elvin Bethea plays both. I like Elvin, and I like the way he plays."

For many years, All-Pro seemed like an impossible dream for Alzado. Rich Jackson and Paul Smith won the honors during Lyle's first few years, and by the time he started achieving some recognition on his own, the Broncos switched to a 3-4 defense.

The three defensive linemen on the 3-4 are usually outnumbered, sacrificing themselves so that the linebackers can be free to roam. Very seldom do you find a defensive lineman on a 3-4 team making All-Pro.

The idea of making All-Pro burned like a flame inside Alzado for years. He had just about resigned himself to the fact that he would never make it.... Instead he'd simply try to do the best job he could, and watch other people get the honors. But then, in 1977, he was picked on the combined consensus All-AFC-NFC team. He often wonders where he'll fit in when the great defensive ends of the modern era are discussed.

"When I first started out, I couldn't estimate my chances of lasting in pro football. I didn't know whether I was good enough, just like I don't particularly think that I can ever be the greatest defensive lineman who ever played this game. I don't think I'm talented enough.

"I'm not stupid; I know what I am and what I'm not. I'm not going to tell you I'm going to be the best who ever lived. Just wait and see, because I'll work harder and harder. I know what the limits of my talents are.

"A lot of things that take place on the football field don't come naturally to me. I hustle and I work hard, and that's why things happen for me sometimes. But the really great ones are the guys who had it come naturally and then worked hard at it besides.

"It bothers me a lot, but I give it my best shot. If there's anything I want to be remembered for, anything at all, I want people to remember that when they watched me play I went to the ball, no matter what happened. I always hustled, I always worked hard out there. That's what I want to be remembered for. I've been All-Pro, a hard working All-Pro.

"You always think about being the best football player you can be, but what makes people think you're the best football player in the league when there are so many great athletes on every team? Sometimes I feel that when they pick an All-Pro team, they should pick an entire side of the defense—like me and Tom Jackson and Randy Gradishar and Steve Foley. I mean it's a tremendous honor to have something like that happen, but I think it's very difficult to choose one guy and say he's an All-Pro. There are a lot of intangibles: the people next to you, what they're doing out there, how they're helping you. What I'm trying to say is that it's a combination of a lot of things. I don't think one man makes an entire defense.

"I say that because maybe I'm just not talented enough to be that good. I'm not a technician. I'm a *street bum*. I get out there and I fight. I try to do the things I'm supposed to do, but I get in there and I go... Well, sometimes I just lose my mind a little bit."

NINE:

Lyle Alzado: A Coach's View

Lyle is like a Rocky Marciano. He beats the hell out of them, and finally he starts getting through there.

—Stan Jones

STAN JONES, the Broncos' defensive line coach, is a youthful 45, curly-haired, and—at 220—30 pounds lighter than he was in his playing days. He lasted 13 years in the NFL, mostly with the Chicago Bears, and in seven of those years he went to the Pro Bowl, both as an offensive guard and defensive tackle. He played against some of the greatest offensive and defensive linemen in football history. He was Lyle Alzado's first coach during Lyle's rookie season of 1971. Then he left the Broncos for four years, returning in 1976.

"During the four years I was at Buffalo, Lyle used to call me almost every week," Jones says. "We would talk about problems he was having, and I'd try to help as best I could, but over the phone you can't do too much.

"When I came back—well, in a way Lyle was like a son whose father had been away for a while. When Papa comes back, the kid wants to show you what he can do."

What Alzado showed Jones was intense desire and a knack for making big plays, "for making things happen," as Jones says. Lyle had become the kind of player Jones was able to rate with the great ones he'd seen and played against.

"Lyle is one of those crucial players. It's always important for him to be in the game. My view is that a superior defensive lineman ought to be a factor in every third or fourth play from scrimmage. He ought to be doing something, causing something. He may not make the tackle, but maybe he's closing a hole and forcing a guy to go to somebody else, or he's hit the quarterback, or he's made an assist, or he's made a tackle. He's *doing* something. And Lyle is *always* doing something.

"It's not just that he's defeated a block and pursued. He's always around the ball, and he's a factor all the time. He's very consistent in this over a long period. He's never varied very often. Oh, sometimes he'll have a couple of plays—three or four—but then all of a sudden he'll spurt. But overall, in the 50 or 60 plays, he'll look okay in the game. He'll be a factor once out of every 3.5 times, or better.

"As a coach, I don't like to give grades based on mistakes. That's just encouraging people to play it safe. If you go by just a plus or a minus—well, it's a good way to grade offensive guys, but not defensive.

"Rich Jackson made a lot of mistakes when he first started. His negative grade would have countered any great thing he had done. So when I got into this, I told him, 'Let's forget the negatives, Rich. Let's not worry about it. Let's just see how many great plays you can make. I want them to think pluses.'

"I'm talking about actually doing something in a game that's measurable—covered a fumble, caused a fumble, sacked a quarterback, flushed a quarterback—some measurable thing about which I can say, 'It's not just whether or not he met the block right.'

"For instance, a defensive lineman who makes a tackle on the screen, who makes a tackle on the draw, no matter where it is on the football field—well, that's a big thing for him to be able to do. That's a real plus. On running plays in his area, at this point, he ought to be able to make a tackle at 3.5 yards or less. I mean, if the ball gets into his area it's second in six, and that's something we don't want.

"I fought pretty damned hard to get Alzado early in the draft. I was all set to take him in the second round. Most people were thinking of him in terms of being an offensive guard. They felt he wasn't quite the size of a defensive man, and he didn't quite fit into what they felt was the mold. They felt you'd have trouble trying to get him into some very disciplined type of defense, and maybe it was true.

"I think Lyle would admit that he hasn't always been as disciplined as he is now. And in some ways he could probably play in a four-man line better than he does in our own 3-4. But he feels now, and I'm sure we all do, that it's the team thing we're after. The team concept is what we've had success at.

"After I saw films of Lyle in college, I talked to Whitey Dovell, our offensive line coach at the time. He'd seen Alzado in person. I've known Whitey since 1949; we played college football at Maryland together. In fact, we were really old friends. He said, 'Stan, he's your kind of guy. I guarantee it, no question. He's everything you thought he'd be.'

"Lyle has great endurance. He goes, I guess, as hard as anybody who ever played the game. At the beginning, he did it through guts more than natural ability, but he was rough around the edges.

"People ask me if Lyle is really a mean guy, a street fighter. They ask if he really spits on guys and everything. I tell them he's pretty damned rough, and he packs a lot of punch. His speed, plus his strength and everything—that alone is enough. But I never saw him do anything to maliciously hurt anybody in my life. He doesn't give what I think of as cheap shots. He's never been a cheap-shot guy. I've never seen him ever do anything that was any worse than what 90 percent of the people in the NFL do. He's a very intense guy, very sensitive, but the intensity he plays with is almost scary. He is really psyched up.

"He has his own program mapped out, and sometimes his program is not mapped out to our program. For instance, earlier this season he wanted to start on the top page, and he got discouraged about not getting a lot of sacks. Of course, our defense doesn't really lend itself to a lot of sacks from the linemen. We don't have a four-man rush on the passing. We don't put four linemen in there and rush on passing downs, like New England does. Our 3-4 defense doesn't lend itself to a lot of sacks, and yet he was playing well at the time—even without all the sacks.

"And he's doing a lot of pursuing out there. He's

making a lot of tackles in pursuit because most teams are naturally right-handed. They'll run their plays to the right side, *away* from Lyle.

"He'll play well against Neely on Sunday. He's much stronger than Neely. But on pass-rushing, Lyle's problem is a lot like Rich Jackson's was. He doesn't finesse it quite as much as Deacon Jones did. Deacon would ignore the men he played against, and go right for the quarterback. The man in front of him was nothing; he'd just go by him. He'd get off such a quick start, like Fred Dryer and a lot of guys who get off so quick they just run their man. They'll run them like Pat Toomay does. I had Toomay in Buffalo, and a guy like him will run them and then do it with movement. They'll create movement in the offensive linemen, and they'll use that movement against them, and it's a finesse type of thing. It's a timing and a feeling. But they don't really physically do a whole lot with them.

"Now, Rich Jackson was more like Lyle. He'd just knock his man apart and gradually wear the guy down. Lyle is similar to Rich in that he's like Rocky Marciano: he beats the hell out of them and finally he starts getting through there. If he had enough pass-rushing opportunities, he would eventually be making a lot of sacks. But with our offensive situation, we were seldom way ahead, so that the other team had to throw a lot.

"I think that not making All-Pro for so long probably bothered Lyle more than any other guy I've ever worked with. I used to tell him, 'Lyle, you do it off of a good team; you've got to have some team recognition first.' There's a guy from Chicago who called me at the end of this year and said, 'You're getting a lot of publicity out there. What's happening? You have a guy by the name of Al—how do you pronounce his name?—Alzado?' Now, that's Chicago, and we played Chicago a year ago.

"You get certain people in pro football who get a reputation, and they get lodged in there at All-Pro and

Class of '67: A senior at Lawrence High School, Long Island.

Varsity days at Yankton College, South Dakota, 1968.

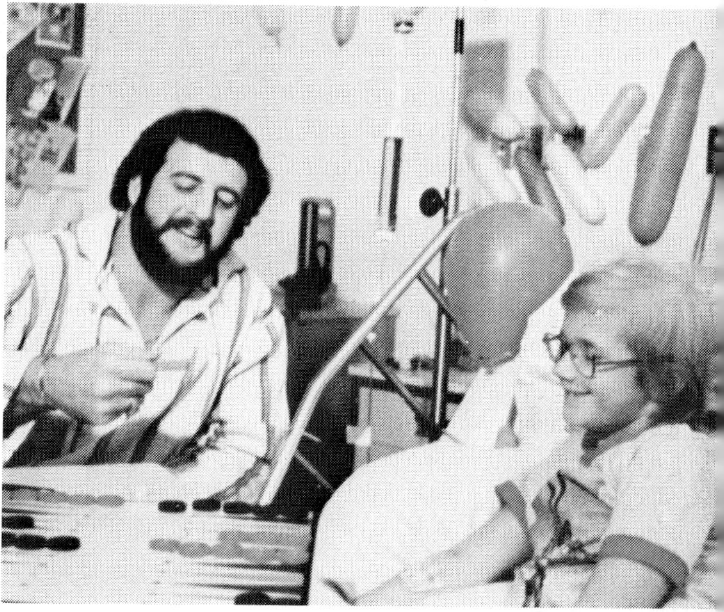

Bed-bound backgammon: a '77 visit to Denver Children's Hospital.

With the special
Special Olympics kids — May 1975

The Alzado family at home in Littleton, Colorado, for Christmas, 1975: Wife Sharon, Samoyed husky Bronco (naturally!), and Lyle.

A September '76 injury put Lyle in a cast for eight weeks and off the field for an entire season.

Lyle and his mother, Martha in New York – June 1972

Stunned, his body spent from the ordeal, Denver's Lyle Alzado sits on a foot locker following the team's 27-10 loss to the Dallas Cowboys in the Super Bowl.

they come from pretty good teams, and they just keep making it every year. But players are guilty of this, too. When they pick an All-Pro team, they'll pick a guy with a name. They're worse than we are.

"They don't even know who the guy is. Everybody thinks an All-Pro team picked by players has to be great, but I've been in there. I *know*. Sometimes you walk up to a player in the hall and say, 'Who have you played against this year? Who gave you a hard time?' Now, is he going to say Joe Blow, the guy nobody ever heard of? He'll pick a big name; to build himself up by saying he played against somebody super. He isn't going to pick a guy nobody knows and say that guy beat him. That will make him look like zilch.

"In the history of defensive ends, Lyle would rate in the upper echelon, and against the run he might even be in the upper tenth percentile. He's a better end than Deacon Jones against a run, and he might be as good as Gino Marchetti against a run, too. I'm prejudiced, but I think the best end against the run in the history of football is Rich Jackson. I don't think there's ever been an end against a run any better than Rich. I can show you some of the things he did against a run, and I would say Lyle is in that category. Unfortunately, ends make it, because... Like Harvey Martin, they get to the quarterback. They make twenty-six sacks.

"And the thing is that Lyle is just super against the run, and he makes some of the damnedest plays there. But unfortunately, it's a pass-rushing thing, and he's a good pass-rusher but not a great one. A guy like Toomay is a great pass-rusher, but he can't play the run at all.

"Toomay came to us from Dallas, and the thing they said about him was that he could play the run but he wasn't a good pass-rusher. They took him out in pass-rushing situations. He was the run guy, and Too Tall Jones was the pass-rusher. I would have done it the other way around.

"Lyle is definitely in the upper echelon of great

defensive ends, but I think the best I ever saw was Doug Atkins. I knew Doug real well; we were teammates on the Bears. Doug wouldn't go full throttle every play, but his half throttle was better than most guys' full throttle. He was like a dinosaur, 6-8, 270 pounds, with 18-inch biceps and 16-inch forearms. I mean, he was just massive. He high-jumped 6 feet 8 inches in college and then worked out for track. An amazing guy. He would run with our receivers; he could catch a ball, dunk a ball. He was drafted by the Lakers.

"We used to play volleyball down by the goalpost, and he could actually spike the ball over the crossbar. You don't find that kind of God-given talent. He was a dinosaur, and you don't see those. That's physical. Lyle Alzado is a great player, but God just didn't give him that kind of equipment."

TEN:

Always the Knee

I never think about getting hurt during a game, because when you think about it, that's when you get hurt. You start playing scared. But when you see a guy hurt on the field and you have all that time to stand around... well, of course you think about it. And everybody's thinking the same thing and they're lying if they say they're not. They're thinking: Thank God it isn't me.

—Lyle

IT HAD escaped Lyle Alzado for five years, that most dreaded of all injuries—the knee. One season the Miami Dolphins was decimated by nine knee operations. Even the most hard-bitten of football people are appalled by the dreadful toll knee injuries take on the game every year. "The knee. Always the knee," Vince Lombardi once said.

Being in fine physical condition means little when your knee is hit the wrong way, when your cleat catches in the turf and forces an unnatural movement, when you make the sudden wrong twist. For Lyle Alzado it came in 1976, just as he was reaching his peak as an NFL defensive lineman. He was finished for the year. It was tough on him, tough on the team—and tough on his wife. The fear of the unknown is always there: the fear that you'll never come back.

Lyle remembers: "I tore my knee on the opening play of 1976 against Cincinnati. I was the nose man, the middle guard. After Paul Smith got hurt, they installed me as the nose man.

"Playing nose guard is like riding the subways in New York, nothing but people bumping into you. On this first play, the guard came down when I was in pursuit, hit me in the center of the leg, and my leg got caught on that Astroturf. It's funny because I didn't actually feel anything. I went back to the huddle and I felt kind of sick—when you hurt something, hit your funny bone, you feel ike you want to lie down a minute and just go *uhh*, you know?

"I went back to the huddle and looked up at Randy Gradishar and Randy said, 'Lyle, you're all white. What's the matter?'

"I said, 'I'm just nervous. It's opening game and I'm just really nervous.'

"So I got down in my stance on the next play and Johnson, their center, came out at me. I tried to hit him and I fell down backward, right on my back.

"I said there's got to be something wrong with me. Then I jogged off the field. Dr. Leidholt walked over to me, he looked at my knee, and said, 'Walk up and down for me.' I did it, and he said, 'You're through, that's it.' I said, 'What do you mean?' I thought he meant just for the game. He said, 'You're out for the year. It's your medial collateral ligament.' And that ended that.

"When it happened I couldn't believe it was that serious, because it didn't hurt. But when they put me under anesthetic for the arthrogram they said, 'You might be in a cast when you wake up,' and, 'If we don't have to operate we'll have you in a brace.'

"When I woke up I was in a cast, and then I knew it must have been serious. I called Steve Antonopolis, our trainer, and asked him what I had to do. He made me do isometrics, even with the cast on. I did hundreds and hundreds of isometrics every day. When I got the cast off I only had a quarter of an inch, maybe half an inch of atrophy in my whole leg.

"He would hold me down on my ankle and on top of my knee, and I'd push up lying on my side, with the cast. I'd do a hundred up this way, then I'd lie on my back and do a hundred up that way.

"I didn't have any pain, none at all. Steve told me he thought my threshold for pain was pretty high. So that's why there was never any pain. And he worked me out, three hours or four hours a day.

"I think that, anytime you have an injury like that, they're afraid you may not come back and they look for people to fill in. Knowing that, I used to start to work out early in the morning. Steve would meet me at 6 or 7 in the morning and get me out of there before anybody came, and I'd be out again by 9:30. I felt embarrassed to be seen working out. I didn't want to meet anybody. People avoided talking to me about it. I don't think anybody liked seeing something like that, because it could be the end of a guy's career.

Always the Knee

"There was no doubt in *my* mind that I'd come back. I told Steve every single day, 'I'm going to be back. I'm going to be as good as I can possibly be. I'm going to try to be as good as I was in '75 before I got hurt.' But really, there was no telling. I wanted to make myself believe, without any doubts, that when I did come back I wouldn't have any of this thing in the back of my mind—the thought that, well, if I get hit, I don't know what's going to happen. When I started my rehabilitation, minus the cast, I'd spend the same amount of time on it—two or three hours. Steve would work me out on what we call the Cybex machine. You strap your leg in there and it measures pounds per pressure on the graph. You strap your leg in, from the ankle to the top of your thigh. And Steve worked me out on that thing. I never missed a day, not even Sundays.

"It didn't get boring; I looked forward to it because I wanted to prove that I could come back and play. I wasn't through playing yet.

"I got thousands of letters. And my wife, she went crazy opening them up, cards and all. I got cards from the kids I work with at Children's Hospital, from the police departments, from everywhere.

"From September to November Steve wouldn't let me do anything except work out on that Cybex. And then all of a sudden, I think it was the middle of November or so, he said, 'I want you to run today.' Afterward my leg was so sore from running I couldn't believe it. But by the time camp opened, I was ready.

"During the time I was out I thought about other possible careers. I started doing a sports show on radio in Denver called 'The Salt and Pepper Show,' with Billy Thompson. I got better as it went on—went from bad to not so bad. But I was uncomfortable, talking to a microphone, realizing there are a lot of people out there listening to you.

"I remember calling Tom La Sorda, 'Tom Sorda,' and pronouncing Bowie Kuhn, 'Bowie Kahn.' I got a call from somebody who told me I didn't deserve to be on the radio... 'If you don't know how to pronounce names,' and so on and so forth. Anyway, they paid me $800 a month to do it."

It was a tough period for Sharon Alzado. She had lived through Lyle's triumphs and disappointments on the field; through his constantly changing moods. But this was something different. It was a continuing profound depression that didn't lift until Lyle knew for sure that he could come back from the operation. She had never before seen him suffer a serious injury, but this time she had had a premonition.

"It was the first game of the season, and I was watching it on TV. I know this sounds unbelievable, but I've never watched a Bronco game alone in my entire life. I've been with friends or had people at my house. That day I woke up and had this terrible premonition that something was going to happen.

"I got up at 7 in the morning, very upset, and I just had the feeling something was going to happen to Lyle. I prayed for an hour that Lyle wouldn't get hurt, that he'd come out of this game injury-free. I was supposed to go over to someone's house—they had invited me over to watch the game—but I stayed home alone, all by myself, and the first play of the game Lyle was hurt. I just knew it. The minute he was hurt I thought, how did I know this was going to happen?

"I don't believe in anything mystical like that; it's never happened to me before. But it's the only game I ever watched alone, and I just refuse to watch a game alone again.

"The worst thing was thinking about what it was going to be like for Lyle. He'd never had an injury—high school, college, never. I kept thinking, what is this going to be like for him, mentally? Will Lyle be able not to play a whole year, to just sit on the sidelines?

"It was awful: the first half they didn't say what was

wrong with Lyle. But I didn't see him in the second or third play of the game, and they didn't say anything about him, so I didn't realize he was hurt until after a while. I thought, my God, what's happened to him? They didn't even announce on the national coverage that Lyle was hurt and out of the game until the second half. So I really wasn't sure how bad it was.

"Then everybody called me and said, 'What happened to Lyle?' I finally tuned in to a local Denver station. They announced that it was serious and he probably would have surgery and be out the whole year. And right away, the only thing I could talk about was Lyle's mental state. I didn't even care about his knee or his leg because I knew that would heal. But I didn't know if he could get over it mentally.

"He got back from Cincinnati that night. I picked him up at the airport and we took him right to the hospital. He wasn't bad before the operation. His spirits were a little higher, he laughed a little. But after surgery he got into this terribly depressed mood. And of course the next game was just unbearable for him.

"He went to the game and stood on the sidelines, which is against NFL rules. You're not allowed to do that. So he was told he'd have to leave the sidelines and find a seat in the stands. He never went to another game the rest of the year. He watched them on TV.

"I was there at that game. My parents were in town, and we all sat together. Lyle knew about where we were sitting, so he looked up at us at halftime and motioned to us that he was leaving. We got up and left to go home too. We watched the second half on TV, which was really hard.

"I always say that if something like this ever happens again, I think I would rent a second apartment somewhere else. It was really hard. You had to watch everything you said. At first I waited on him hand and foot; anytime he wanted something I'd rush to his side. I did everything for him, and then as the time got on I finally realized I couldn't do it anymore. He took most of his frustrations out on me, which I guess is natural. But at times it seemed like he didn't like anybody.

"He'd yell a lot around the house, but he didn't break that many things. He was very clumsy with his crutches. Things got broken because of his clumsiness, not because of his rage. Most of his rage he kept inside. I wish he had let it out a little more. But what bothered me most was that the cast chipped up all our toilet seats. We had to replace all the toilet seats in the house.

"He was very ashamed of the injury; it was almost like he was in hiding. But he worked out continually. From the moment he got to the hospital he started leg lifts. He didn't miss one night, no matter what kind of mood he was in. Then they put on one of those new casts that has hinges. He could do all sorts of things. They'd move the little hinge each week to give him more mobility in his knee. So when he got his cast off, his knee was in better shape than it had been before.

"I went with him the day he got his cast off, and they tested it for mobility and strength and size, and it was amazing. They said they'd never seen anything like it. He had recovered much better than anybody they'd ever seen. He was killing himself working out, lifting weights all the time. But I guess it paid off."

ELEVEN:

The Dirty Dozen

We could never win the right games; we could never win the big games; we never beat anh playoff teams. Coach Ralston just wasn't a good coach. It was as simple as that.

—Lyle

JOHN RALSTON arrived to coach the Broncos in 1972, fresh from eight straight winning seasons at Stanford and two impressive Rose Bowl upset victories.

"Our goal is winning the Super Bowl," he said when he arrived. "There's no question that we'll make it; the only thing is that we don't know how long it will take."

Ralston's first job was curing a sick passing game, since the Broncos had never had a high-level quarterback. He traded for a cagey veteran, Charley Johnson, and drafted a future All-Pro tight end, Riley Odoms, in the first round. The passing game added nearly 500 more yards. Scoring, which had been close to the bottom of the league in 1971, was up 122 points.

The defense, which had been solid in 1971, slumped a little with the departure of Richie Jackson, but in 1973 Ralston picked up Ray May—a strongside linebacker and an inspirational on-the-field leader. The Broncos made national TV with their practice of holding hands in the huddle, a practice introduced by May. It was fine with Ralston; he was a Dale Carnegie man who liked to win friends and influence people. He believed in positive thinking. Pretty soon the defense was back, and a team whose record had been 4-9-1 in 1971 and 5-9 in Ralston's first year, now—in 1973— had its first winning season ever: 7-5-2.

By 1976 the Broncos—with a flamboyant, free-wheeling defense—were closing in on their first playoff spot. Jim Graham, a veteran Denver columnist, went down to the airport to watch the Broncos return from a successful trip. He leaned over to Gordon McKnight, the chairman of the Broncos' Boosters' Club, and said, "This man Ralston is another Vince Lombardi, nothing less."

New England ended all playoff hopes with a crushing 38-14 defeat in the season's 12th game. The Broncos finished the season at 9-5, best in the club's history, but there were storm warnings. In a game in Houston, offensive coach Max Coley—the X's and O's man on the field—had gone to the hospital shortly before kickoff. Ralston was in a fog during the game. He couldn't handle the technical details and the offense collapsed: 154 total yards, six out of 23 passes completed. The Broncos lost, 17-7, and a very striking impression had been left with the players—Ralston simply didn't understand technical football at the professional level.

They knew they had the material for a Super Bowl, but they felt that with Ralston there they would never make it. Seeds of revolution had been sown, and hidden resentments against Ralston—always a popular figure in the city and in community affairs—began surfacing.

For Lyle Alzado, they traced back to his second year, when Ralston burned out Richie Jackson by forcing him to scrimmage on a postoperative knee. And he had had his own personal problems with Ralston. One year, Lyle has asked to leave training camp to clear up some "personal financial matters." Ralston denied him permission, saying "No, I'll take care of it. I'll call some people and have it taken care of." But he never did.

"They were basically financial problems. There were some bad checks I had to cover for my family, and they could have been in big trouble. I had moved my family—my wife and sister—out here to Denver, and they needed some money.

"It was a thing that could have developed into something really bad, and I needed to have it taken care of right away. He wouldn't let me leave. He said he'd take care of it, and when I got back it was twice as bad. Other guys told me he had lied to them a lot, but they never went into detail.

"About that time a lot of guys started wondering about Ralston. The Broncos had been laughed at by everybody. We had gotten used to playing for a team that didn't have any respect. When you talked about the Denver Broncos, you automatically said the word 'doormats.' And it was true. Hell! We used to win four or five games and thought it was a good deal.

"When Coach Ralston came he drafted a lot of talent; he brought a lot of talent to Denver and did a lot of things to help the organization. But we could never win the right games; we could never win the big games; we never beat any playoff teams. In some ways, Coach Ralston was a good man. He just wasn't a good coach. It was as simple as that.

"I don't know why he double-crossed me that one time. I don't know whether he got lost up in training camp and forgot about it or what, but it never materialized. It hurt me because he called me in the office when he first took over as coach, and I told him I wanted to be the best football player in the world. He told me he thought I had the potential to be a Merlin Olsen. And after I walked out of the office I thought to myself, 'Merlin Olsen! There's no way in the world I have the natural ability to be like him, to have his style. Now why would he tell me that? He could have said 'Lyle, you can be the best football player you want to be.' That would have made more sense.

"Before the Dirty Dozen thing broke, we had gone in to meet with Ralston and had asked him for changes. We wanted a quarterback we could win with. Steve Ramsey was there, and Steve Ramsey would come off the field laughing when he threw an interception. That annoyed a lot of us. I remember once, last year when I was hurt, I met with a guy on the team and had a drink with him and asked how things were going. He said, 'After that New England game when we got beat up there, Steve Ramsey threw an interception and came off laughing. The guys wanted to punch him in the face. The guys told Ralston about it but John just let it slide.'

"Ralston changed nothing. We asked him for a

number of things and he changed nothing. We talked to him prior to the 1975 season. We went 6 and 8, and got beat in Miami 14-13 on a blocked field goal. We went in and talked to him about a month after the season ended. We asked him to please get us a quarterback, and to please help us win. We wanted a new defensive line coach, and we wanted to get Stan Jones back here. Well, we got Stan back in '76, but it was Fred Gehrke—the personnel director—who brought him back.

"Who were the Dirty Dozen? Well, there was me, Billy Thompson, Billy Van Heusen, Paul Smith, Tom Jackson, Riley Odoms, Otis Armstrong, Rick Upchurch, Louis Wright, Tommy Lyons, Mike Current, and Haven Moses.

"The twelve of us got together after the '76 season and drew up a petition. We called everybody on the team and the petition ended up with 36 or 37 names on it. The club said we had no right to do what we were doing, and a few players felt we had gone about it the wrong way, and I feel today that maybe we should have gone about it in another fashion. But we were hungry for the Super Bowl and we knew we had the material for it.

"We had a press conference. The petition said we no longer felt Coach Ralston could lead us to a championship, and we felt that under his leadership we could not go any further than we already had. Some people say we should have brought the petition to Gerry Phipps, the owner, but instead we just called a press conference. Maybe that was a mistake. Mr. Phipps—who has been good to all of us, and who in my opinion is a great owner—said not to release it, so we didn't. But one guy left a press release there for a reporter to find, and it was released.

"I don't know if he did it deliberately, but it was a mistake. A very big mistake, because we promised Mr. Phipps that we wouldn't do it, and it caused a lot of pressure for the organization, which we're very sorry for."

The player who had left the petition was Bill Van Heusen, the punter and backup wide receiver. He was cut from the Broncos the following season, and no other club picked him up. Some players felt he had been blackballed by the league, but his 35.3 average—in the thin Denver air which adds yardage to all kicks—put him in the NFL's lower rankings.

Resentments formed among the players, resentments that still existed below the surface even during the Super Bowl season. Jack Dolbin, the split end, was among the Ralston faction, although he later admitted that, in retrospect, the end result had been positive. Jim Turner, the kicker who had played for Ralston in college, got on television after the petition incident and said, 'These guys have set pro football back 20 years.'

The wildly partisan Denver fans—and their Boosters' Club—were a bit stunned, but Boosters' Chairman Gordon McKnight says that, looking back on it now, he should have seen it coming.

"Last year, in retrospect, was a pretty disappointing season," McKnight says. "Everybody had huge high hopes when the Broncos went to New England. It was all right there in front of them. They controlled their own destiny as far as the playoffs were concerned. And they laid a horrendous egg.

"The team had the softest schedule it had ever had, and everybody predicted the playoffs for sure. They went 9 and 5. I personally was a big John Ralston fan, and it's obvious now that John brought a lot of talent to the football team, but as the players pointed out, he was not capable of coaching them on the field. But when the player revolt took place, it was appalling. It was like a businessman having his employees kick up their heels, so to speak."

The club was not to be railroaded. Gerry Phipps

announced that Ralston would stay on as head coach, but Ralston had had it. On January 31 he resigned and went to work for the Dale Carnegie Institute. One day later the Broncos announced the hiring of Red Miller as head coach...Red Miller, who had knocked around the NFL for 17 years as an assistant, never getting a shot at the top spot.

"When Mr. Phipps announced that Ralston would remain as coach," Lyle says, "we figured we were all done. I asked to be traded to St. Louis. I don't know why, but I always wanted to play for them. We decided individually what we should do and just did it. Most of the guys ran for the mountains, ran for the hills. And when Mr. Phipps asked for an apology, Billy Van Heusen was the only one who went. They obviously figured he was the leader, and he wasn't. I don't know why only he had to apologize. I would tell who the leader is but if I did it would destroy his career, and I won't do that.

"But things did change. Fred Gehrke was named to take full control of the team, as far as draft was concerned—players decision and movement of players, trades, that kind of thing. Fred Gehrke got Stan Jones back. John never wanted Stan back. Fred Gehrke kept all the defensive coaches here, and he was responsible for all the offensive coaches, too.

"Looking back, maybe it was a mistake for us to go about it the way we did. We wanted to do it with respect and with honesty. But it didn't turn out that way. We should have listened to Mr. Phipps and gone about it the way he planned. However, it worked out for the best. We got a great coach here, Coach Miller, and we're all happy. Finally we have the respect of the league.

"I'll never forget my first impression of Red when he walked in the first day. He gathered everybody—the doctors, the trainers, the players, the owners, *everybody*. He got up in the room and said, "Good evening, gentlemen. I'm Red Miller.'

The Dirty Dozen

"We all looked up at him, waiting for the next thing, and he said, 'One thing I want to get clear. When you go over to your meetings, there are soda-pop machines and candy machines around there. You stick the quarter in, you take out a pop or a piece of candy, and you go in the meetings drinking your pop and eating your candy. I don't want you to do that. I want you to concentrate.' He paused for a minute and then turned around at the blackboard. Then he said: 'AND I MEAN IT!' We knew he meant business. He had our attention from then on.

"For instance, when you're late for a meeting you get fined. You're supposed to be there on time. So I was late for a Friday meeting. I was like five or six minutes late.

"The room was dark and I snuck in there. Then we went out to the practice field, and I was hoping he didn't see me. I was loosening up, and he walked over to me and looked at me and got up real close next to me.

"He said, 'Hey, Lyle, were you late for the meeting today?' Smiling, patting me on the shoulder. And I wanted so bad to say, 'Not *me*, Coach!' But I looked at his eyes and said, 'Yeah, I was late.'

"He stopped smiling, got a real serious face, and said, 'That will cost you a hundred dollars.' And I said, 'If anybody wanted to take a hundred dollars from me he'd be in for a hell of a fight.' First time in my life I ever gave away a hundred dollars nice and easy."

TWELVE:
A Tough Business

Toward the end he started telling me what it was like, how much stress and strain a player is under. He's like a puppet in the organization—a piece of meat, that's all he is—and when they're through with you they cut you and let you go. And he got banged up more as he tried harder; and after the game he'd come home full of tension and mad. He became so mean and hard I was scared of him.
 —Roxanne Gay, accused of fatally cutting the throat of her husband, former Philadelphia Eagles' defensive end, Blenda Gay.

THE MYTH is that winning cures all troubles, that a winning team is close and everyone gets along. The Yankess of 1977 changed a few popular ideas; the team won the World Series even though it was undercut by personal resentments and recriminations that bubbled beneath the surface all year and often came to light.

Any collection of extraordinarily talented people is subject to that, any collection of super-egos. And in football, where many of those talented people have a faintly concealed substrata of violence, the results can be even more striking.

Innocent jibes are often resented. Too much attention by the press and public is resented. The Denver Broncos are no exception, which Lyle Alzado found out the hard way. He found it out early in his career, when a young wide receiver pulled a gun on him in a team meeting. He felt its effect later when the player he had been closest with gradually drifted away from him, and when the defensive players got together for a party—having failed to invite him. It drove him deeper into himself; it affected his wife and his friends.

Lyle Alzado sits in the weight room at the Broncos' practice site in 1977, telling an out-of-town newspaperman the story of his early life—the fights, the violence. As he speaks, Godwin Turk—a reserve linebacker—throws an orange at him. It barely misses his head. He picks it up, curses, and charges into the players' lounge, seeking revenge. Several players yell at him for disrupting their break. He returns to the newspaperman with a smile on his face that soon disappears.

"A lot of these guys don't particularly like me," he says. "I play this game with a lot of emotion, and I think it turns off some of my teammates and people around me. But I never pretend I'm something I'm not. I'm a moody person, moody because of the game, and maybe because of my background. The game puts me through a lot of different emotions. It's something I can't change.

"I guess I'm a loner, a guy who doesn't get close to people. I have few friends because a lot of my so-called friends have betrayed me. My best friends, the guys I've been closest to in my life, are all guys from the old neighborhood; from Long Island.

"I know my weaknesses, I know what's wrong with me, I know what my problems are—but I admit them. I'm short-tempered, I'm moody, I'm disliked by a lot of people because I am emotionally intense, but that's the way I'm doing it. That's the way I think I have to do it. This is the way I believe I've got to do it to be a successful football player.

"I don't particularly think I'm the most popular guy on this team, and I don't mind that because I understand how they feel toward me. I like the people—I mean, we don't all get along, but I respect them as football players. There are people I like, people I dislike, but I don't hang around with anybody socially on this team because they know I'm just so intense about this sport. Maybe they also resent the publicity I get.

"Of course, I've got to be part of the team. But I'll tell you what you do: ask the guys I hang around with socially what the problem is. They'll say, 'I don't know.' They probably don't want to say anything bad about me to a reporter, but you ask my wife and my friends. I've always been that way."

Paul Smith, an emerging superstar when Alzado joined the team, is now the left end on the second defensive unit. He has also been Alzado's roommate for the better part of half a dozen years.

It's only the second time the color line has been crossed in roommates on the Broncos (Floyd Little and Fran Lynch were the first). Close friends at first, Alzado and Smith are now polite to each other. They have similar habits; it's an arrangement of convenience.

A Tough Business

In September the defensive team got together for an impromptu party. Alzado was not invited. There is some resentment against his never-ending stream of publicity, against the fact that he is always a focus of attention for newsmen.

"Lyle knew about the party. He was told about it," Smith says. "He just couldn't make it." He looks away. There is no conviction in his voice.

He is more comfortable telling the old Alzado roommate stories.

"We've been roommates for the last four or five years, I guess," he said one day in pre-Super Bowl week. "Rich Jackson was my roommate, but when he left, me and Lyle got together. We hit it off real well from the start. All those old jokes, you know—Lyle said he didn't mind me being his roommate as long as we don't use the same shower; I said, 'Well, as long as you don't eat candy bars... And don't wreck the room like you always do and get nervous before the game and tear the room up.'

"Lyle was a little bit more secluded when he first came into the league; young guys tend to be insecure, especially playing for a coach like Lou Saban. You don't know whether you're going to be here from one week to the next. I remember one time Lou cut half the kickoff team: some guy ran a kickoff back for a touchdown against us. That keeps you on the edge.

"Saban was real good at scaring people. He'd holler and scream in the meeting rooms, and it was his way of getting things across to you. But I really can't say I appreciated it. When a guy made an error, he'd get a phone call the next morning and Saban would say, 'Bring your play book.'

"Before a game I just leave the room and let Lyle tear it up by myself. He wrecks the room. Before we check out of this hotel, the whole room will be destroyed again.

"I think the worst he did to a room was at the Denver Travel Lodge, a few years ago when he threw the lamp and it cracked. He just tore the room up. He's calmed down a little bit in his old age, but he still gets uptight and nervous before a game—like we all do."

It's a smooth rendition of the street-fighter-on-the-road epic, but there is a lot unsaid when Paul Smith talks about his roommate. The defensive party is quickly dismissed—even Lyle Alzado is hesitant to talk about it—and his wife, Sharon, admits to a certain embarrassment about the whole affair. But it put pressure on her, too—pressure she'd already felt as the wife of a public person.

"I don't know if we should talk about it, but once they gave a party for the defensive linemen and Lyle wasn't there. There's a lot of jealousy on any team where one person gets more publicity than the others. It's a group of very competitive people; they're competitive on all levels.

"So Lyle isn't included in a lot of things because a lot of guys are jealous of the things Lyle's getting. Lyle likes them all and he's close to them on the team, but he doesn't see many of them socially.

"He's very sensitive, and if people don't include him or don't like him he outwardly says, 'I don't care. I'm a loner I don't need it.' But inside he's really hurt.

"The party was last September, before the season started. Lyle had missed a whole year of football with his injury, and then to come back in and not be included by his teammates—well, it hurt. And you know what whe worst thing is? Lyle missed an entire year, and the defense last year was great; they were great without Lyle, and that was hard on his ego, too.

"Then he came back and rose to the top, and they're calling him the leader of the Orange Crush defense. And all of a sudden the teammates think, 'Well, gee, he wasn't even here with us last year and all of a sudden he's getting top billing.' So I can see where people would be jealous of that.

"Last September Lyle came home one day—my

mom and dad had just arrived from South Dakota, in fact they had only been there a few minutes—and Lyle walked in the door and gave them a hug and kiss. Then he got very pouty, and naturally we wondered what was wrong. The phone rang, and it was one of the defensive linemen on the team calling. 'Well, Lyle, we're all having a party,' the guy said. 'If you'd like to come, why don't you come on down now?'

"Apparently when Lyle left the locker room he heard them all talking about it, and finally when he left he couldn't resist. He said to them, 'Well, have a nice time tonight, all you guys.' They knew he was aware of the party. Then when they called and invited us Lyle said, 'No, that's okay. I'm not going to come now, not as an afterthought.' But he really felt bad. When Lyle and I have any type of a party we usually include everybody on the team.

Part of the problem is that Lyle Alzado has never been known to duck any newsman's questions. He has always been very decent with the media, and at times—in the pro-football psychology—this is not always fashionable. The Redskins, for instance, have a back door to their locker room, and any players who wish to make a quick exit after a game, to avoid the reporters' questions, can do so easily. In fact, they are even encouraged to do so at times.

"There's only one newspaperman I won't talk to," Alzado says, "because he wrote an article pitting Barney Chavous, the defensive end on the other side, and me against each other. He didn't back it up with facts and quotes, and it stirred up animosity and trouble. I won't talk to that guy."

"What if he came over to you and apologized for writing it?" someone asked Alzado. His face brightened.

"Well, then, everything would be forgotten and I'd talk to him again. Of course I would."

He has thought a great deal about the publicity he gets, and his attitude is: I live my life my way. I choose to cooperate with the media, and if people don't like it, that's tough. It's a philosophy born of the many years when he was nobody, a non-person. He has seen many ex-players drift into obscurity.

Football players live in a sort of dream world during their careers. It's a real world only for a short time, and they think it lasts forever. That's a mistake. For a lot of people it's very, very short. Some people play a long time, but they never adjust to the world. But Lyle is aware of the ephemeral nature of sports fame.

"George Saimes played for 14 years with the Buffalo Bills and Denver Broncos—safety man, fullback—and he was a hell of a football player and a super guy. But I don't think he saved very much money through his career or made one investment.

"He ended up with nothing, had nothing; he ended up a scout. I don't know what he's doing now because I haven't seen him in years. I know people like Mike Adamle and a few people throughout the league, Dan Pastorini, some good people—Phil Villapiano, Jack Ham. But I really haven't been close with that many people."

In the NFL players adjust to the endlessly changing spectrum of faces—friends who are cut, players who get traded, people who just disappear. But it's something that wives can never adjust to. A trade is announced—two names on a piece of paper, a notation on the League TWX. For the wives it means a home disrupted, friends who disappear and are never seen again. For Sharon Alzado it's a personal thing.

"I can't get real close to people on the team right now, because I don't want to lose them. It just hurts too much to have the people you care about most leave. So most of our friends are outside of football. Lyle warned me about that our first year here.

"The first friend we had, Jim Kreig, we got to be close with him and his wife, Peggy, and then he just didn't come back. I was really upset about it. Lyle sat me down and said, 'Sharon, in this game people are going to come and go. We may come and go. You can't get so involved with somebody that you're going to cry for weeks when they leave.' It didn't help. I still got close to people.

"On April Fool's Day the local radio station put it on their news that Lyle was traded to Chicago. Lyle found out about it—somebody told him about what he'd heard on the radio—and Lyle was so upset. He called to tell me and said, 'I'm not coming home,' then he took off and went driving in the mountains. This was last year on April Fool's Day. It had just been an April Fool's joke.

"Finally he called Danny and Paula Davis— Danny's a friend of ours, a disc jockey—in the middle of the night and told them. It came with no warning; he couldn't believe nobody bothered to call and tell him. And that's when he was recovering from the knee operation. It upset him so traumatically, and then to find out it was just a dumb April Fool's joke. Paula Davis said Lyle called the Bronco office, and they wouldn't confirm or deny it.

"When Tom Graham was traded, he was hunting on his day off. He was driving back and heard it on the car radio. And Jeff Severson, when he was traded to St. Louis, was up skiing. He called our house and said, 'Hey, how are you doing?' And I said, 'Oh, Jeff, we're going to miss you so much; I don't know what we're going to do without you.'

"He said, 'What are you talking about?'

"I said, 'Didn't you see the *Rocky Mountain News* this morning? Didn't they talk to you?'

"He hadn't even seen it. His picture was in the *Rocky Mountain News* article about his being traded to St. Louis, and he didn't even know it. So I told him. I think John Ralston was in charge of telling him, but I don't know.

"Jeff didn't believe me. He said, 'Let me talk to

Lyle.' Lyle told him, and he said, 'Let me talk to Sharon. I'd believe Sharon before you, Lyle.' And he said, 'Is this a joke?' I said, 'Jeff, go buy a *Rocky Mountain News*.' He didn't believe us.

"If you worked for a company they'd give you some time to get to a new place, and in football you have 24 hours. The player has to go within 24 hours, and then the wife has to pack up and move the family, house, kids everything, all on her own. You don't even get paid for the full expenses. You get something like a couple of hundred dollars for each state line you cross, so it doesn't come near meeting your expenses. And you have no warning. You're just gone, and I think that's the cruelest part of it.

"In '74, during the strike, a lot of players and their families suffered, too. Like John Hufnagel, a young quarterback. He really had no choice about staying out. If he wanted to make the team he would have to go to camp.

"So he did, and his wife, Penny—a very close friend of mine—was very upset. Lyle and the other players were striking, and it was the first exhibition game, against the Jets. To get into the game we had to go through the picket lines, and it was so hard. Lyle looked at me and said, 'Don't come in the door I'm picketing at.' And all his friends said, 'Lyle, your wife's going in that game. Don't you have any control over her?'

"I was hiding behind Penny, but I said, 'Penny, you got me into this.' That's the first time we ever sat on the 50-yard line at a game, too. The stadium wasn't very full at that game.

"Lyle wanted to play football, so he wanted that strike to end. He was part of it, but he didn't want it to ruin the whole football season.

"Sometimes I think this whole football thing is a crazy dream world, nothing close to reality, and it just puts people in a false existence. When our friends have

A Tough Business

been cut it's been traumatic. I think the team should have a team psychologist or psychiatrist to help make adjustments for the players—instant fame, instant money—also to deal with them when they're cut or traded. The players themselves simply go through too much trauma."

It hits them in different ways. One rookie wide receiver, who broke in with Alzado in 1971, cracked up under the pressure and pulled a gun on Alzado in a team meeting. Lyle's memories of that evening are vivid.

"We had this rookie wide receiver named Dwight Harrison—he's a cornerback with Buffalo now—and one day when I was kidding around with him, I asked him when he was going to catch some passes. He said, 'When you get the quarterback ten times.' Evidently I'd really made him mad. I just turned and walked away, and he took a chair and broke it over my back. So I turned around and beat the hell out of him. This was in the locker room before the meeting.

"He left the locker room and came into the meeting with a gun. Larry Jackson and Marv Montgomery persuaded him to go into Coach Ralston's office and talk to the coach about it, and he did. They got the gun away from him, and the next day he was traded to Buffalo and we got Haven Moses. He had done the same thing to Rich Jackson once and Floyd Little, pulled a gun on them. It was loaded, of course, but I didn't get scared of something like that. Why should I? It's happened before.

"I've had a gun pulled on me before. I've had knives thrown at me, that kind of thing. I haven't been afraid of very many things in my life. I've been afraid of being lonely. That happens a lot. Even now. I tell my wife, and she puts me in her arms and tells me that it will never happen. Believe me, meeting that woman is the best thing that ever happened to me.

"A lot of things are so hard on her, things I never

hear about till later. A player's wife came over to the house once, and she and Sharon were talking, and all of a sudden she said some other player's wife had said, 'A lot of guys are mad that Lyle's getting all this publicity.'

"And Sharon said, 'Well, Lyle's not asking for it. People come to him because they're interested in him. Lyle sometimes gets annoyed because he gets interviewed so much.' Which is the truth. I do. But I try to be polite to people, and I try and give them the respect that *I* want.

"About a week later the same lady called up and said, 'Gee, my husband never got recognized when he came off the field and came out of the locker room after the Oakland game. Lyle got all the publicity: he was on national TV, Larry Merchant, and so on and so forth.' She was telling this to my wife, and here's my wife having to defend me again for something people want to know about me. That's not exactly fair, is it?

"I don't particularly like being a public figure now. There are a lot of rumors that start; there are a lot of things people say about you that aren't true, things they think about you that aren't true. My teammates also. They think I do one thing and their wives think I do another thing.

"Sometimes they'll come over to my wife and say, 'We heard Lyle was fooling around with this girl.' And it's not true. Things like that.

"Why do rumors start anyway? Why do people love dirt? I think that, subconsciously, everybody is jealous if somebody else has more than they do. And I think when that happens, if they hear the slightest thing, I think they enjoy the fact that something is hurting that person who has more than they have.

"I don't think they do it on purpose. When I got hurt, there were people who were glad I was hurt because now they had the opportunity to try the things I usually do. When I see somebody do something I want to do, I'm jealous of it and say, 'Maybe if he screws this interview up, or if maybe he does something on the field...'

"I was very jealous when Harvey Martin got Defensive Player of the Year, because I was in the running. The Mack Truck Award. Of course I'm jealous, and I was hoping they didn't think well enough of him and they thought more of me. That's a natural part of being human, and I'm not going to deny that. But at the same time I think that if you keep it in perspective, with respect to other people, it's fine.

"I don't particularly think making everything public and being loud in the crowd, so to speak, is the right thing to do. I think people have the right to be and act in a way that is truthful to themselves—as long as they don't hurt anybody.

"There are only a few people I can talk about this to. I really have maybe one good friend in Denver, and he's not even an athlete. He's a disc jockey, Danny Davis. I don't have many people in football that I'm close to. Steve Zable is one, but I never see him. He plays for New England. That's why it's lonely for me. Now that I'm going to the Super Bowl, all these people are coming out of the woodwork, people I haven't seen for years asking for tickets.

"I don't mind it though, that's fine. My wife gets very upset with a lot of this stuff because she knows what I sometimes do for people, and she knows how I always get stuck in the ass or slapped in the face for it. But I don't ever think I'm going to get disillusioned with people, because I need to be around them too much. I need to feel people too much. I don't think it will ever happen. At least I hope it won't.

"I want the people that count to remember I gave them the real part of me, and that I did it the way I thought was right to do. I was nothing else but me. I was never phony.

"I saw an article on me in a Chicago paper this week.

The writer said he didn't know whether to believe my old fight stories, and he thought I spent more time in the barroom than the classroom. All he has to do is call up some of the people in the old neighborhood; they'll tell him the truth.

"What I am is what I am. The image that is portrayed through other people's eyes and other people's words is the way they want to see me. So if something is written or said or done, I can't go and tell people to erase it, because it's done. It's been said. How do you change that? You don't. I'm really most interested in being true to the people that mean something in life: Sharon, Red Miller, Stan Jones, Jack Martilotta, my brother Billy, Don Birmingham, the guys I hung around with in Long Island, Danny Davis."

Occasionally an image is brought back out of the past, something that catches Alzado up short and sends shock waves through his body—something from the distant past, when he was fighting for his life on the streets of New York.

It happened after the Broncos beat Oakland for the AFC title. Dave Frei, Denver's assistant PR man, received a call from someone who said he was Lyle Alzado's father. He left a number where he could be reached. He asked him to tell Lyle to return the call.

"Lyle looked shocked when I told him," Frei says. "His face got white. He took the number, but he looked like he was in shock. I didn't know what it all meant."

Sharon Alzado knew only too well what it meant. Her husband's past was trying to cash in.

"We were out celebrating at the Colorado Mining Company, a restaurant in Denver, and Dave Frei—the public relations man—came in and said, 'Hey, Lyle, I've got a message for you. Your father called the stadium asking for you.'

"I could just see Lyle's heart sinking. I said to Dave, 'Is this a joke?' Lyle hadn't heard from his father for 12 years or more. And Dave said, 'No.'

Tears came to Lyle's eyes, and he just left the table. So I thought, I'm going to leave him alone for a while and let him think this out. Then I'll go talk to him. I knew he was real upset. I went to talk to him and said, 'Well, Lyle, what do you think you should do?'

"Here's the man who neglected Lyle, never cared whether he was dead or alive in the last dozen years of his life, and now, all of a sudden, Lyle's Super Bowl–bound and here's his father again. That's the way I look at it, but I didn't grow up with him, so I don't know. If he'd have called Lyle even two months before that it wouldn't have been so bad, but the timing of this call was terrible.

"Anyway, Lyle never returned the call, but I'm sure Lyle would like to see him again. I'm sure he feels that. I really think Lyle would like someone to be proud of him.

"You notice how most people who make it big in life—actors especially—never seem to have a father figure in their lives. So many of them don't. That's one reason I think my dad and Lyle are really close. My dad's more a friend than a father figure, but it's somebody who can be proud of him. And I think he needs that. I think he'd like to see his father, yet he knows how much his father hurt his mother and the rest of his family. Lyle went through what he did because of his father.

"You know what I find hard to believe is that other people don't relate to this. So many people assume I live with this brute who throws me around the house. Outsiders think that mostly. In Denver they don't because everybody sees the humanitarian side of Lyle. He gives every ounce of his spare time to charity, and he will not say no to any autograph-seeker. He bends over backward to please people. I hate that, when people think I'm married to some big animal.

"Lyle draws so much on his past, a little more than I think he should. But I think that's part of him. I can't relate to that, but I still try to understand it. As Lyle puts it, I will never fully understand because I never had to live that kind of life.

"When I was visiting him in New York, I would go for a walk by myself at night, and I would take off by myself and walk down West Broadway or whatever it was. One night Lyle came running after me and said, 'What are you doing, walking alone? You don't walk alone in New York; you don't walk alone in this neighborhood.'

"I don't like to hear him bring up his past because I think it just brings up sadness. It's true, he brings it up, and I think that's a need that he's always going to have. I always thought if he saw his father and went back to where it was and got it out of his system, he might not have to bring it up anymore. But it's a part of him I can't get rid of. I would like him to start thinking about the present and the future rather than dwelling on the past.

"People think Lyle is still a street brawler, but he's lost most of that. People can only push Lyle so far, like if we're out in a crowd or somebody does something. Not in Denver, though. I haven't really seen him lose his temper quite as much in Denver as I have when we went back East, where nobody knows him. I've seen his temper flare, and I've seen him jump out of the car and run after somebody because they tried to do something. But I've never really seen him in a huge fight.

"Sometimes people who don't know Lyle ask me, 'Doesn't he scare you?' He doesn't. I have never had to fear Lyle. His father used to beat his mother, and Lyle was so repulsed by that that I don't think he would ever hurt me. When I first met him, this guy could kill me with one blow. I always was afraid of that, but I'm not anymore.

"Lyle's very moody. His temper doesn't upset me as much as his moods. He can go from one mood to another in a second. Like tonight we were driving over to Antoine's, and all of a sudden something upset him. His mood changed just like that. Then he got over it."

THIRTEEN:

What Next?

I think my wife would be happier if I were a more private person, if I didn't spread myself so thin. But there are so many people who need help. I'm not a religious person, but I believe God has something else planned for me in this life; I don't think he just wants me to be a football player.

—Lyle

IN 1977 Lyle Alzado won the Whizzer White Award for the NFL player who had done the most for community affairs. He could have won it every year since he joined the Broncos, because community affairs have been his life away from the field.

His own financial security was assured almost as soon as he joined the club. His first contract was for three years at $18,000, $22,000 and $27,000 per year, with a $12,500 signing bonus thrown in. But with the emergence of the World Football League, NFL contracts took a big hike, and general managers—fearing the loss of players to the rival league—quickly sat down and renegotiated contracts. Alzado soon found himself propelled into the upper levels of the pro-football salary structure. The last contract he signed put him at $100,000 a year with extra bonus packages possible for All-Star honors.

It wasn't tremendous money, compared to the NBA and major-league baseball, but for football it was decent enough. And in Sharon Alzado he had a shrewd financial planner, whose investment instincts had been finely honed by years of working at her father's credit bureau back in South Dakota.

Alzado loves his work with the 20 or so Denver charities that carry his name on their letterheads. He especially likes his work with handicapped children—handicapped physically and emotionally. But sometimes he toys with the idea of a career in football coaching. Football is a tough business to get out of your blood.

"My daydream is to get a coaching job at a big university—Michigan, someplace like that—and pick my own coaching staff. Sometimes I can even see myself as a defensive line coach.

"The things Stan Jones did for me, the things Jack Martilotta did for me, and Sal Ciampi and Richie

Mollo... I wouldn't mind doing the same things for someone else. I know the hours are long and you wind up looking at those films into all hours of the night. I did nothing else but live in the street and stay up late and foul up; maybe staying up late will help me do something good.

"My wife would have me around more because I wouldn't be traveling so much. She'd know where I was; she could go with me and share things with me. I don't think I could coach at the high school level, though, because it would frustrate me now that I've been exposed to so much football.

"As a head coach I would try never to lie to my players. I'd try to be straight with them. I'd want their respect more than anything else. I might have trouble cutting guys, benching guys who are trying hard but just aren't good enough. It would be very difficut for me, but I'd have to be honest—I couldn't tell a kid he had talent if he didn't. I'd like to copy Stan Jones' knowledge and emotional togetherness with his players. And in some ways I'd like to be like Red Miller—the rapport he has with his players, the honesty and straightness he has with us.

"Red's put my whole career back together for me. He called me into the office when he took over as head coach. I was one of the first players he called in, and he said, 'You know, Lyle, I want to win here. I want to win big here. If you want to be part of this organization, if you want to be part of my club, then believe what I'm telling you. Don't question me. Just do what I tell you, we're going to win.' The thing that he has is to be able to get inside you.

"Red told me he thought I could be the best end in football. He said, 'As long as you work hard and concentrate, you're going to do it.' And he's helped me this year to be just that.

"Red will even go into techniques with defensive guys. He'll go right down into the pit with you. He's a pretty tough guy, unbeaten as an amateur fighter. Very strong, too. One day a 250-pound center named Kenny Brown went over to him and put his hand around his neck and made a wrestling motion at him. Red threw a move on him and Kenny threw a move on Red. Red countered it and put him on his back. Twisted him like a pretzel.

"Once Red got down and tried to show Claudie Minor—280 pounds—a technique. He went at Claudie and Claudie went at him and Claudie's face bar cut Red on the forehead. And there was Red, finishing drill with blood running down his face.

"Maybe that's the kind of coach I'd be, but maybe I'm being unrealistic, too. As I said, maybe it's all a dream."

Sharon Alzado listens to all of this and nods. But she knows coaches, and she knows her husband, and she finds only a remote connection between the two.

"Personally, I don't think Lyle has the temperament to be a coach," she says. "Not even close. Lyle is so individualistic, and coaching is regimentation, isn't it? But I can't tell him that."

She sees life in community affairs as more realistic ("Lyle says he's not a businessman, and I agree with that"), and at times she welcomes a life away from the public microscope. She is patient about letting him take his time and make up his own mind. The only thing she asks for is relief from the pressures that weigh on their lives now.

"He isn't really sure about the future. He wants to use his special education to work with the handicapped as more of a charitable thing than a career, and I'm sure he'll do that. He got into a radio show with Bill Thompson of the the Broncos, and he enjoyed that thoroughly. Every year he's tried something different. He leased cars one year, he did PR work for a New York firm—all sorts of things.

"Now he's got lots of business opportunities. We

even considered moving back to Yankton and starting a racquet club or health spa. They need one desperately, and the people there would go crazy for one. It's a beautiful city on a beautiful lake and we could live a very nice, private, relaxed life. And the cost of living is so low.

"Every year Lyle plays it by ear. I think the best thing that happened when he was injured was that he realized football doesn't last forever. That was the only reward we got from that part of our lives, the fact that Lyle realized he would eventually have to do something besides football. So we've done a lot of thinking on it.

"But his popularity in Denver now is really at its peak. Somebody ran a survey on the street in Denver: 'If you could meet anybody in Colorado, who would you like to meet?' Eighty percent of the people queried ansered, 'Lyle Alzado.'

"He's just a public figure. Everyboy in Denver knows Lyle. Maybe it's because he's got a name like Alzado, and he's got a mug you can't forget—I mean you see Lyle's face and you just never forget it. But kids love Lyle, and he's really great with kids—all ages. Even babies are attracted to him. We'll go somewhere and kids will flock around.

"As far as the way all this affects me... Well, I've gone through so many stages in my life. First I was very jealous of all this attention he got. Then I went through a resentment stage where I resented all the people out there taking from him. Now I'm at the stage where I take it in stride and I don't mind. I understand that he is a public figure, and that these people who flock around him are making him what he is right now. If he didn't have any fans, he wouldn't be where he is now, and neither would the whole sport of football.

"But it's very shallow, and I don't like it mainly because we don't have a private life. We can't go anywhere without Lyle being swamped for autographs. If we go out to dinner people sit down at our table. I go to the grocery store and write a check and everybody gushes, 'Are you Lyle Alzado's wife? Oh, the Broncos are doing great!'

"So I carry cash a lot because if I write a check or use a credit card everybody starts to talk to me or about Lyle. I realize everything I do reflects on Lyle. Like if I'm in a terrible mood, I can't be rude to anybody, because then they'll say, 'Oh, that Lyle Alzado's wife is a real bitch.' *Really*.

"One day I ran into the grocery store with my hair in rollers. I didn't have enough money so I had to write a check. I wrote out the check and they said, 'Oh, you're Lyle's wife.' Then as I was walking out, I could hear, 'Oh, Lyle Alzado's married to *her*. Gee, he could have married somebody better-looking than that.'

"I can't go into the store looking like a rag. I have to look nice because I'm representing Lyle and everything I do reflects on Lyle. I don't have a very private life. Our phone rings off the hook; we get our number changed every year but still somehow people get it. If the phone isn't ringing the doorbell's ringing, people dropping in at all hours. Everybody says, 'Oh Sharon, you lead such an exciting life.' Granted, it's exciting, but it's also very hard. It tests our relationship. Sometimes I just don't feel like sharing Lyle with the world.

"And it's shallow. When he stops playing they're going to say, 'Lyle who?' It's just going to end. Just like Floyd Little right now. He was one of the most wonderful players the Broncos ever had. He *made* that franchise. All of Denver loved him. And people don't even remember the name Floyd Little. Floyd is a forgotten man as far as his teammates and the public are concerned. He's not playing anymore, so he's not a public figure. That's just the way it is. When Lyle stops playing, he'll still be active in the community, but he's not going to have everything at his fingertips—people buying him dinner and drinks every time he goes out.

"All of a sudden Lyle has all these people just crawling out of the closets. High school friends he hasn't seen or heard from for years, hardly remembers how to pronounce their names, they're suddenly calling him. Here's a perfect telegram we got last week: 'Hi, Lyle. Hear you're having a great season. Remember the old Lawrence days?' On and on, all in a telegram. And then at the very end, the last line, 'We could use four tickets to the Super Bowl... let us know.'

"Hasn't even seen them, you know? People Lyle hasn't heard from in years, just calling to cash in on the big thing. Friends we've never seen, all your big buddies. Like at the hotel here tonight: he's had calls from people he doesn't even know, but they're all his friends now.

"People in college... The worst thing about Yankton College was the way they made fun of Lyle. He worked out so hard, saying I'm going to be a professional football player.

"Nobody drafts anybody from Yankton College. You don't become a professional football player by going to college with 500 students, so a lot of these guys made fun of Lyle. They said, 'Oh, you'll never make it.' And those same guys, they call us in Denver, they want to come out to the game and they pat him on the back. 'I always knew you could do it, Lyle.' And they're the ones who got out there and spit on him when he was trying to make it.

"But Lyle totally forgives all of them. Lyle's such a forgiving person. That's one bad trait of mine, I do not forgive very easily. It takes me a while. If somebody does something really bad, to Lyle especially, I don't forgive them. I hate to see Lyle hurt. It really upsets me."

South Dakotans are self-reliant people, and Sharon's father, Bill Pike, sees Lyle as a person who's tough on the field but soft in his personal life; soft on those who make demands on his time, on his emotions. He finds it difficult to reconcile the many conflicts in Lyle Alzado's personality.

"Before a game he simply closes himself in, isolates everybody," Bill Pike says. "Maybe that's a part of his being tough. I couldn't do it. You've got to be associated with people; you can't tie yourself up in a knot and avoid everybody. But that's what he does.

"When he first started going with Sharon, none of us were aware of all this violence in his background. We knew he was from the East, and that was it. We didn't know anything about this other stuff. Neither did Sharon. Things still come to light that were unknown to her. But I don't think it would have bothered us one way or the other, because after you get to know him he's a nice person.

"It's a little surprising that he's so sensitive. I've given him some lectures a couple of times within the last year, because I think he's gone too far in letting all sorts of people use him. He lets people take advantage of him. A cripple asks to use his blazer and uses it for two days. I don't think this crippled man has any right to do that, take advantage of another person. I told Lyle, 'Tell him to just forget it.' Help people in general, but don't start helping individuals. Once you take on individuals you're sunk.

"I put it in the form of a note to him after having talked to him about it, because he didn't answer one way or the other. So I wrote him a note. He put it in with his socks, where he keeps everything important. I gather it meant something to him.

"I want him to stay with four or five charitable organizations to keep the name up, but I don't want him to get personally involved with this handicapped person or that poor broken-down person, because two or three people like that can just drain all your time. I've told Sharon, 'When letters come like this tear them up and throw them away, don't let him see them.'

"Lyle doesn't want her to open his mail when it's addressed to him. That's a bad thing. My wife, Edith, and I have always believed that everything is ours, period. There is no his or mine or hers.

"Lyle and Sharon have never had any major fights. Maybe when they were going together they had a little spat or something, like when she was working at the Kennedy Golf Course and she went out with the pro there a couple of times. Lyle came after her one night when he knew she had gone out with the golf pro. He grabbed her and took her out of her own apartment and said he didn't want her seeing John anymore.

"I felt this way: if he harmed her in any way I would actually come to Denver and—who knows what would happen then? I wouldn't let any physical harm come to my own daughter. But I don't think that would ever happen. I really don't feel he would ever physically harm any person he likes or loves. He's really got a deep emotion that way.

"Look at the way he helps all those handicapped children. Yankton is where he first got interested in helping those kids. He had a real soft spot in his heart for them. I find it hard to relate to because I have never been one to devote big blocks of time to somebody else's troubles, so I really don't understand why Lyle devotes so much of his time to it. I dish out a few dollars, but I'll be damned if I'll do what Lyle does. I went through the WPA days with my dad and we worked our way up from the bottom, so I get a little tired of people complaining all the time about their troubles. And I just don't know why Lyle, who pulled himself up from the bottom, didn't say, 'The hell with it, you guys pull yourselves up, too.' I just don't understand that.

"Handicapped kids—OK, fine—that's a fine group to work with. But Lyle gets calls for assistance from damn near everything out in Denver. That's the worst part. If you were with him during the off-season you wouldn't believe it. He's gone five nights a week, doing this and that and talking here and there.

"He used to do it for free, but he quit that after the first year, when he found he couldn't do it for nothing all the time. Now some things he does for free, some are paid, but the fees in Denver are just $150 to $300 usually. He'll go out meaning to stay for an hour and a half, but he usually spends four or five hours.

"It's funny: I've known Lyle for five or six years, two and a half years really closely, and I still don't fully understand him."

It's a complicated problem: how much of yourself can you give to others? With Lyle Alzado, a lot of the solutions are governed by instinct—the same instinct that guided him when he saw those handicapped children playing kickball in the Yankton gym.

He feels most comfortable, most needed, around children. And he knows how to handle them, how to handle himself around them. The petty jealousies of life are pushed in the background. He sees his own past and he remembers the way he regarded adults: two types, phony and straight.

"I find there are a lot of kids you see and talk to who want to understand why they should change. They ask, why not go out and steal something and not have to work for it? They say, 'I don't get anything out of working anyway.' They feel tougher if they take something. No one's going to tell them what to do. I say, 'Look, the only way you're going to succeed in doing anything is to care about yourself. If you don't care about yourself, stay in the hole you're in. Don't bother me with it.' Sometimes they listen, sometimes they don't.

"I've gone into classrooms and talked to kids and been laughed at. And I've walked into classrooms where they sat and listened. I've had kids come over to me and say. 'Hey, Lyle—thanks, man.' You know,

'Can I call you sometime?' I'll give them my home number, and they'll call me or I'll get together with them. But sometimes they walk over to me and say, 'You're full of shit.'

"But I can relate to the bad-ass kids. They look at me and say, 'He came from where I was.'

"Sometimes they believe you and sometimes they don't, because when they look at a professional athlete they think, 'Well, it's been handed to him.' But it's not always that way. Some of the kids listen and say, 'Wow, can I do what you've done?' I can't tell them, 'Well, work out.' Maybe they don't have the ability to do what I've done. I say, 'You don't have to be an athlete. Be something else. I don't care if you're a garbage man, but be the best garbage man on the block. Make people respect you.'

"That's what I was always taught. I picked garbage all through school, trying to make money and stuff.

"When I lived in the streets, my friends would say, 'Lyle, don't ever be anything else but what you want to be. Because when you act like something you're not, people disrespect you when they find out.'

"I've gotten involved with some kids in real trouble. I've had phone calls from different supervisors, asking me to come talk to different kids—sometimes athletes. I went to one school and sat down and talked to the kids about what had taken place in my life, what's taking place in their lives. I told them I would give them a ticket to a Bronco game if they would raise their grades one notch. If it was a D, they'd have to raise it to a C, or from a C to a B, or from a B to an A, and it turned out so well that I didn't have enough tickets. But Mr. Phipps came through and gave them the tickets. All of them raised their grades, like 20 kids.

"Maybe I should cut back. That's what my friends and family say, but how can I? I'm going to cut back a little bit, but I won't cut back much because I know

What Next?

how happy I can make some people. I think it's very unfortunate that athletes who have the opportunity to be something and do something with people, to give them something they've never had before, don't do that. It's selfish.

"I'm actively involved in about ten kids' programs: the Special Olympic Program, Police Athletic League, Multiple Sclerosis, Muscular Dystrophy, the Untouchables—that's a group that helps kids from ages of 8 to 19 who are on drugs. And I work with the National Jewish Hospital in Denver.

"I work with the police, too, in a delinquent control capacity when they need me for something like... Well, when there were racial problems at one school in Denver, Thomas Jefferson, the police asked me to go over and help calm the kids down, to talk to them.

"When I got there a lot of it had calmed down, but it was still very tense. There had been some beatings, that kind of thing. The first thing I did when I got there, when I faced any of the kids who walked over to talk to me—especially when they recognized me—was to make sure I didn't try to make myself out to be better than they are.

"I didn't want to say, 'Hey, come here man, let me talk to you a minute about something here.'

"Because you're a professional athlete, or a professional writer, or professional broadcaster, they'll look at you and they'll automatically think, 'This guy's better than me.' That's it, right there, that's how it starts out.

"You want to walk up to the kid and say, 'Hey brother, what's happening? What's the problem?' You let them rap to you, let them rap it out. I said, 'Well, that's cool. If that's what you feel you've got to do, do it. But you're just going to destroy yourself, and if you don't care then I don't care either.'

"When I left it was a little better. There were a lot of policemen around there, social workers who helped out. I wasn't the only person.

"Another thing the group I work with—Delinquent Control, under Lieutenant Lou Lopez— does is visit schools in Denver and throughout Colorado to help stop the flow of drugs into schools. Once I even carried a gun, but I never came close to using it. I had a .38 Special then, a .357 now.

"I fail all the time, too. But once in a while I don't, and that's what counts. I can feel those kids. I know what they feel like because I was there. I know what they're thinking; I know what they're feeling.

"They think, well here he is. He's got money, he's a professional athlete, he's in the public eye, he's doing this, he's doing that—and they don't care.

"I remember the time I went to a school in the Five Points area in Denver, and I walked into the classroom and it was black, a little bit of white, Mexican-American—and I got up and started talking to them. Half the class went to sleep, three or four walked out, and the others just talked with each other. I was destroyed. But a week later I walked into a classroom where three or four listened and maybe only five left. But if three or four are going to listen to me, then fine, I'm a winner.

"None of the kids I did reach and help actually came back to look me up, but I have run into kids later. I'd be at a specialty track meet for the mentally retarded or something, and they'd come over to me and say, 'Lyle, I remember meeting you. Thanks for talking to me and taking time with me.'

"I remember one kid I actually tried to adopt—a black kid in Denver. I was just about to go through with everything when I found he had a mother in California. It started one night when he was 16. He came over to my apartment and asked me to give him money for a bottle of liquor. I didn't do it, and he walked out mad and everything. After we worked things out we spent time together, and he said, 'Thanks for not giving me that money.' That was a couple of years ago.

"You don't try to be better than they are; you try to be what they are and try to relate to them. A lot of guys come off trying to be better than they are, and naturally they don't like it. It does help to come back to them more than once. Coming back always means more. The first time they think it's just a token visit, but if you came back they think you really care. They start believing you.

FOURTEEN:

Broncomania

> *It was unbelievable: the cars trying to drive down the streets couldn't move; players were being pulled out of cars; Craig Morton was almost dragged out of his vehicle....*
> —Gordon McKnight, Chairman of the Broncos' Boosters Club, describing the parade after Denver beat Oakland for the AFC Championship.

IT HIT a victory-starved town like a spring flood from the Rockies. Broncomania. Denver had never had anything like it—a team in the Super Bowl. The Bronco fans waved their little orange banners and their orange shirts and their placards in the stadium, in the streets, and later in New Orleans, they took the city by storm. Orange, the gaudy color of those who had been deprived, according to one psychologist. It was a giddy two weeks of festivity, starting with the Oakland victory and leading up to the Super Bowl. It first hit Lyle Alzado after the Broncos beat the Raiders.

"Right after the playoff game, the fans ran onto the field and ripped the goalpost down and started chanting and banging on the locker-room doors.

"I ran right into the locker room. But after we got in the locker room a couple of the police officers came over to me and said, 'Hey, Lyle, a lot of people out there are screaming for you.'

"So I went out by the door and they grabbed my foot. I couldn't get back in. I had the policemen pulling me from one end and the people were pulling me from the other end—it looked like a gang fight.

"I said, 'There goes my leg.' Then I looked over and Red Miller was reaching down and shaking people's hands. Somebody grabbed his watch. Red tried to slug him, then he grabbed him and said, 'Gimme back my watch, you son of a bitch.' And the guy handed it over.

"I kept thinking, 'We've done it; we've beaten Oakland. Biggest game in the Broncos' history.'

"I was the last one to leave the locker room, the very last person to leave. I must have left two and a half, maybe three hours after the game. I just couldn't leave. I didn't want it to be over. I stayed around answering questions and just realizing what had taken place. What a feeling. What a thing to have happen!

"The questions they asked me: How does it feel? Do

you realize you're going to the Super Bowl? What does the Super Bowl mean to you? Was this the biggest game you've ever played?

"How do you talk about something that's never happened to you before? It's difficult to express. The Super Bowl for the Denver Broncos. Just think about that. We go from 6 and 8 to 9 and 5 to 12 and 2—and the Super Bowl. That's an incredible climb.

"I got calls from all over the country, friends of mine, all with congratulations.

"My insides were so wound up I felt like I was going a hundred miles an hour. I couldn't eat that night, couldn't sleep. I was up the whole night. Every play I had done, I went over and over and over in my head.

"And then, during the week, we had that incredible parade through the city—a ticker-tape parade. Fifty thousand people closed in on the cars, tried to pull us out of the cars. The cars couldn't move, and all these people were grabbing at us."

They had been deprived, and they were making up for it: loyal fans, blue-collar workers mostly, who regularly filled Denver's 75,000-seat Mile High stadium, coming from as far away as Salt Lake City, Omaha, and Mizzoula, Montana. Six-hundred-mile commuters. At one game, 60 no-shows were announced. The fans booed the no-shows.

At the Sheraton Airport Hotel in New Orleans, the Broncos' pre-Super Bowl HQ, the fans started arriving late in the week. A suite was set up to handle them. Daddy Bruce—a 77-year-old caterer who supplies free food to Bronco players and club personnel—always had a golden-brown, aromatic Virginia ham or some ribs, close by. One day Gordon McKnight, an ad salesman for the *Denver Post* and the chairman and upcoming president of the Broncos' Boosters Club, dropped by to sip a beer and talk about the season, about the original growth of Broncomania—and orange as the team color.

Broncomania

"Everybody was apprehensive going into the first regular-season Oakland game. We had won four games in a row, and we went to Oakland and destroyed them, 30-7. The city went crazy. There were 10,000 people at the airport to meet the team. They couldn't even walk through. The players ended up with sleeves torn off their jackets. It was a zoo, and that's when it began. The Orange Crush defense, at that point in time, had legitimately won the game for the offense. The offense sputtered and wasn't really developed until late in the season.

"The way this orange stuff first started: In 1973 me and a guy named Charley Goldberg passed out the first piece of orange to the Denver fans. Charley's a Denver businessman, and he paid for all of this orange material that was passed out. It was just pieces of orange cotton. That's all we could get on short notice.

"Orange wasn't really recognized as the official Bronco color then; it was incidental. The team was in a real rut, and we were under the Lou Saban reign as coach and general manager at the time. Fans were becoming extremely boisterous—throwing garbage on Lou's lawn, insulting his kids, doing horrendous things—and finally his family had had it. He resigned, which made way for the John Ralston regime.

"In 1973, Ralston's second year, we were on our way to our first winning season. The orange thing began to snowball, beginning with a slogan: Big Orange, How Sweet It Is.

"Charley Goldberg and I passed out those little pieces of orange to all the fans. We had 52,000 fans, and we had 35,000 or 36,000 pieces of orange cloth for the fans to wave in the stands.

"We scrounged the material from fabric stores and dry goods wholesalers. A clothing manufacturer volunteered his staff to cut it up into 3-inch-wide by one-foot-long strips.

"The promotion cost about $1,500. Charley

Goldberg footed the whole bill, which he's done a number of other times.

"And then, right after that orange thing, we went out and won two games. After a very bad slump, two big wins. That was a few years after Art Modell voted against the merger, saying, 'Could you imagine having a team like the Denver Broncos play in my stadium?' Well, a year later, in Art Modell's stadium in Cleveland, we beat them 27-0. Both Floyd Little and Dave Costa got on national TV, on NBC, and told what was happening with the Broncos.

"The Orange Crush happened a year ago, when the defense started really playing well after they went to the 3-4, which was necessitated by injuries to a number of the defensive linemen.

"Alzado was out after the first game against Cincinnati, and a couple of other defensive linemen were out, and so they pieced together the 3-4. The linebackers really adapted to it, and if I'm not mistaken, Channel 9 sportscaster Bob Kurtz coined the phrase 'Orange Crush Defense.'

"This year we looked at the schedule and said, 'Oh my God, it's terrible!' But late in the preseason, after we'd gone through six games and were 5-1, there seemed to be a positive feeling.

"After the first Oakland game, all of a sudden the Orange Crush thing came out of the woodwork. People were buying shirts for our home game against Oakland two weeks later, which is the official Orange Sunday every year. The Orange Crush company cashed in on it in a big way. Orange Crush tee-shirts, *any*thing orange started selling. When you got to the stadium it was a sea of orange.

"So many wild things happened during the season. There was a lady who missed her bus to a game. The Regional Transportation District didn't have enough buses for all the people who bought season bus passes to ride to Bronco games. She missed the game, took them to court, and Judge Sanchez ruled in her favor that they had to pay her $44 in expenses. The judge said that, had she asked for more in personal damages, she probably would have gotten it.

"In a bar in one of our worst neighborhoods, a guy was watching the end of a Bronco game. Three guys came in and put the jukebox on, so he pulled the plug. They put it back in. He got so mad he went home and got his wife's handgun, then went back to the bar and shot all three. One of them died.

"There was a mailman who went to a lawyer's office all the time, and the mailman said, 'I'm tired of the Broncos; they're not going to do anything this year.' The lawyer said, 'I don't have season tickets. I'd love to buy yours.' So the lawyer bought them for the season. Come playoff time, the mailman said, 'Screw you, I'm taking the tickets for myself.' The lawyer took him to court, and the judge ruled in favor of the lawyer.

"Then there was the time Steve Cameron—the columnist for the *Denver Post*—wrote a column about a nightmare he had about the color orange. For weeks afterward he received hate mail, crank calls, death threats, the whole thing.

"Some guy in town has an Afro hairdo dyed orange, and he wears a blue and orange suit. At our Christmas Eve playoff game against Pittsburgh, a guy with a beard showed up in an orange and blue Santa Claus suit. Coach Miller even has an orange toilet seat in his house.

"After we beat Oakland in the AFC Championship, the city and state announced there's be a Bronco holiday on Friday, January 6. The governor and the mayor declared it, but then there was a great upheaval when the newspapers got hold of it and reported that this little day was going to cost the taxpayers in excess of $5 million. So they retracted the state holiday. But the governor at one point—and I honest to God heard it on radio—said to the business community: 'Any company that doesn't let its employees off on Bronco Day should be ashamed of itself.' Then he was backed into a corner, and he retracted the day. But there were still a lot of cases of orange flu.

"A good 50,000 people were at the parade after that Oakland game. The parade was supposed to take half an hour, but it took over two hours. It started at the state capitol and went down 14th Street, up 15th, down 16th and back up 17th Street to accommodate all the fans, and it was insane downtown. I happened to be at the office of our secretary of the Quarterback Club, it's in a high skyscraper. I looked out the window, and you could see a vast majority of downtown Denver. It was unbelievable. The cars trying to drive down the street couldn't move; players were being pulled out of cars; Craig Morton was almost dragged out of his vehicle. It was frightening to the players. And after beating Oakland it was terrifying.

"Someone actually bought two Super Bowl tickets in Denver last week for $350 apiece. I know of a Denver oilman who paid $180 a ticket for the Oakland game, and he bought 12 of them—said he'd have bought more if he could have found them.

"The typical Denver fan is a workingman, somewhere between white and blue collar... let's call it a light-blue collar. Some are vicious; most are not. But there's definitely an element of ruthlessness."

FIFTEEN:

One Week to Kickoff

Will swap 2 Super Bowl tix for anything that don't eat.
—classified ad in the *New Orleans Times-Picayune*, Saturday, January 7, 1978

"I'VE NEVER seen anything like this," said James Evans, the sales director at the Hyatt Regency. "Hotels are fully booked for 25 miles around New Orleans. Every day our registration desk gets calls from people, asking about rates. We tell them we're all booked up and they say, 'That's Okay, we just want to know how much to charge for renting a room in our house.'"

A bellhop at the Royal Sonesta smiled and talked about renting two rooms in his house to a group of 10 men. He said he was charging them $25 per head, per night.

"I'm gonna make over $1,500 for the week," he said.

Antoine's, Galatoire's, the Caribbean Room at the Pontchartrain, the Commander's Palace—all the better restaurants have been booked for months in advance. Some took reservations anyway, then told the people they'd have to wait two hours for seats.

Eight days before the game Tony Angello, owner of Tony Angello's Italian Restaurant, on Fleur de Lys, sat at a table off the bar and watched his bartenders working in a frenzy, their arms flying like pistons as they tried to take care of a mob bellied up, four deep, waiting for tables.

"This is only the beginning," he said. "You want the business, but this . . ." He waved his arm expansively in the direction of the bar. "I just don't know how we're going to get through the week."

Wild rumors spread through the hotels, about 3,000 hookers who were going to be imported especially for Super Bowl week. To quell the tide the *New Orleans Times-Picayune* ran a story headlined: PROSTITUTION ARRESTS TOTAL 27 IN FRENCH QUARTER THIS WEEK. The piece went on to detail the 27 arrests in three nights of police scrutiny. No mention was made of the other four nights.

The hunt for Super Bowl tickets became fierce. In

Dallas, where scalping is legal, classified ads during the season regularly carried ads from people wishing to sell tickets for $60, $75, anything up to $100. For the Super Bowl, the sky was the limit. Thirty-eight thousand season ticket holders were allotted 10,000 tickets.

"As you can guess, it's been a nightmare," the Cowboys' PR man, George Heddleston, said. "We've been overwhelmed with calls. They come from all over. The Cowboys are a national team; we have fans everywhere. They want to know what color uniforms we'll be wearing, birthdays, biorhythmic cycles—and always tickets, tickets, tickets."

The wildly partisan Denver fans got an even tougher break on tickets—14,000 of them for 75,000 season ticket holders. Travel agencies in and out of Denver went into the ticket business, and naturally they stuck it to the Bronco fans pretty well.

Two weeks before the game, US Travel—a Washington-based agency—set up shop in a suite at the Hyatt Regency in New Orleans. Their activity was aimed at the Denver fans.

"We'll pay $70 a ticket," said James Didion of US Travel. Never mind that it was illegal to sell—or buy—a ticket for $40 above list price.

"We're paying $30 for the ticket and $40 for expenses," he said. He didn't mention how much he was going to sell them for.

"We've got a new ticket-scalping gimmick in town now," said Joanne Williams, the cashier at the Desire Oyster Bar on Bourbon Street. "Ticket lotteries. It's very big in the neighborhood bars.

"A guy will come in with a ticket and hold a lottery for it, right on the spot. People kick in $1 apiece for a chance at the ticket. The guy could make $100 or $150 that way, but he has to watch out for plainclothesmen."

The classifieds in the New Orleans papers were loaded with Tickets Wanted ads, very few Tickets Available, although the "Swaps" section made lively reading.

"Will swap two tickets to the Super Bowl for Endymion Ball" (a fiercely exclusive Mardi Gras event).

"Will swap 2 Super Bowl tix for anything that don't eat," read another.

The New Orleans Saints' ticket manager, Henry Simoneaux—who also handled Super Bowl ticket allotments—put on a long face as he sifted through the letters on his desk. He got the best break of all—17,000 tickets for the 34,600 Saints' season ticket holders—but he said he could have sold out the 75,000-seat Superdome twice over.

"Look at this," he said, pointing to a letter postmarked Lafayette, La. The letter read: "Need two tickets badly. Charge me whatever you want."

"Every letter says that," he said.

I told him he ought to advise people to just show up and get all the tickets they want outside the Dome 10 minutes before kickoff. I reminded him of all the scalpers who ate their tickets in the rain before the 1970 game.

"It might be raining outside the Superdome," he said, brightening up for a moment, "but inside it'll be 72 degrees and dry—guaranteed."

On Bourbon Street, the novelty shops—which got stuck with a huge overflow of Bear Bryant and Woody Hayes Sugar Bowl tee-shirts and trinkets—started peddling their Super Bowl knickknacks a week and a half before the game.

"A man just walked in with 200 pennants and 200 little Super Bowl jerseys," said Anne McClendon, the manager of the Carrousel Shop. "We got an early start on the rest of the Quarter. We sold half of them in two days. Two dollars for the pennants, $7.50 for the jerseys. The markup is 100 percent."

Next door, at a sex parlor called the X-Rated Shop, they couldn't care less. A girl behind the counter, in halter top and faded jeans, yawned and shrugged when I mentioned the Super Bowl.

"What's all the fuss? The game's not for another week and a half, right?" I told her the date—Sunday the 8th.

"Well, the game's on a Tuesday, ain't it?" she asked. "What is it, the Denver Cowboys or something?"

Jerry Kaiser, a distributor who handles 40 novelty shops in New Orleans, grimaced in disgust.

"They were supposed to get us all the stuff a week and a half before the game, but they blew it," he said. "The Greyhound bus coming here from Buffalo with the stuff never made it. They said they could send it off on Tuesday night, but I told him to stuff it. Not enough time."

At another shop called Image Makers, a man was busy transferring Denver Broncos and Dallas Cowboys decals to the back of tee-shirts that carry a Sugar Bowl logo in front. You could get it both ways.

"I'll give you one of these things for $5," he said. "If you want a Super Bowl shirt without the Sugar Bowl stuff on it, it'll be $6."

Fly-by-night street vending was risky. A city law forbade street peddling of all goods except Lucky Dog hot dogs, flowers, and ice cream.

Almost unnoticed during the week was the celebration of the 163rd anniversary of the Battle of New Orleans, January 8, 1815. Andrew Jackson, bolstered by 2,000 crack-shot Kentuckians ("I have never seen a Kentuckian without a gun, a pack of cards, and a jug of whisky," Jackson said), crouched behind their battlements and leisurely picked off 2,600 British troops, advancing in perfect formation. American casualty figures were seven killed and six wounded.

"Magnificent, is it not, General?" remarked Gen. Carroll, standing next to Jackson and watching the slaughter.

"Yes," said Jackson. "It's magnificent, but it isn't war."

On Monday, January 9, the Broncos arrived by

charter flight. When they got off the plane, people thought it was a local road gang coming in for runway repairs. That's how bad they looked.

"Hey, how do you get to Bourbon Street?" they asked.

An hour later the Cowboys checked in. Neat. Ties and jackets. Smelled nice, too.

"This is a business trip for us," one Cowboy said. "There's plenty of time to enjoy ourselves after the game."

Makes sense, the bettors reasoned. One team is playing in its fourth Super Bowl against a team that's just happy to be here. The betting line jumped from 4½ to 5½ on the Cowboys.

The Broncos did nothing to dispel their first impression. Their hotel, the Sheraton, was usually deserted at night, right up to Curfew. The French Quarter had been getting a lot of action.

"For a guy like Woody Hayes, this might be a mind-blower," said Bronco middle linebacker Randy Gradishar, an ex-Ohio Stater. "They're running around now, but don't worry. They'll settle down later in the week."

The closest thing to an incident in the Bronco camp was the death threat received by fullback Jon Keyworth. It turned out to be from a nutty girl in Denver.

"That's nothing," said one Bronco old-timer. "In the old days, when we'd win four or five games a year, everybody'd get them."

Before the death threat, the big thing was halfback Otis Armstrong finding a cockroach in his hotel room.

"I want a room change. There's bugs in my room," he told Bronco PR man Bob Pack.

"That wasn't a bug, it was a roach," Peck said. "Listen, when the Chiefs stayed in the Fountainbleu for the 1970 Super Bowl, all of them found roaches in the rooms."

"How'd the Chiefs do that year?"

"Beat the Vikings, 23-7."

"Okay," Armstrong said. "Bring on the roaches."

On Tuesday night, Lyle Alzado came to the mandatory team dinner 50 minutes late. Someone asked Red Miller if he'd be fined.

"Ah, what the hell," the coach said. "At least he got here."

Picture day was a riotous affair. Alzado insisted on wearing a blue woolen cap for the team picture. Many of the players had their cameras out, shooting the photographer as he shot them. Louie Wright paraded around in a black fur coat and hat. They frolicked their way through the press interviews.

"On the Jets in '68, Curley Johnson kept everyone loose," said Jim Turner, watching the goings-on through his 36-year-old eyes. "This team has 20 Curley Johnsons."

"We're happy to be here. Man, are we happy to be here," said fullback Lonnie Perrin, sounding one of the pre-Super Bowl's most significant warning signals. The book says you're not supposed to be 'just happy to be here.' You're supposed to be looking toward the game.

"Could it be," said punter Bucky Dilts, "that we're just whistling in the wind?"

"I like 'em loose," said Stan Jones, the defensive line coach. "They play better when they're loose. But I must admit, this is the loosest I've ever seen them."

"This is a team that's new, fresh, happy, excited," said Andy Maurer, an eight-year veteran of three NFL clubs. "It's exciting just being around them. That's our style.

"I played on a team that was all business when they came to the Super Bowl. No false hoorah, no messing around. They came to four Super Bowls that way. The name of the team was the Minnesota Vikings."

"Let me tell you something about loose teams and tight teams," Red Miller said. "One year when I was with St. Louis, we played the Giants, and we were up

One Week to Kickoff

for the game. We were really ready. We came out on the field early to warm up, and in the other end zone was Fran Tarkenton and some other guys playing volleyball over the goalpost.

"They beat us something like 48-10.

"The way I feel is that we did all our hard work on Thursday, Friday, and Saturday of last week. This week it's polish and enjoy. If I didn't think they could get themselves up for a game like this, I'd be insulting them.

"You can only tighten a screw so much. You can only turn it so many times. If you turn it that one last time, there are no threads left.

"On Sunday we want all our threads."

Tuesday, January 10, was Dallas Cowboys' picture day. Ralph Neely, 34, stood in a far corner of the field, submitting to an interview by three or four writers. In five days Neely would play against Lyle Alzado of the Broncos.

Local writers, mostly, were interested in Neely; he is not a focal figure on the Cowboys, but rather an old pro—13 years' NFL experience—nearing the end of the line. He was one of the last Cowboys out of the dressing room for the mass interview session. For a while he hid behind the stands. He doesn't care much for interviews, and the Dallas fans hadn't exactly been kind to Neely.

Once he was a very hot property—a *cause celebre*, actually. The Cowboys wanted him, and Baltimore drafted him, but so did Houston of the rival AFL. He signed a contract with the Oilers. Then Baltimore gave him to Dallas for a fourth-round pick in 1966; the Oilers took the Cowboys to court and the case was resolved when Dallas gave Houston a first-, second- and two fifth-round choices for Neely in the 1967 draft. That's how much the Cowboys wanted this 6-6, rawboned All-American from Oklahoma.

He paid them back handsomely. He made All-Pro

for four straight years as an offensive right tackle, and then his life took a downward turn. Rayfield Wright emerged as a budding star, and they installed Wright at right tackle, switching Neely to the left side—a traumatic switch for an offensive lineman.

He broke his ankle in an off-season motorcycle accident, and when he came back he became a holder. The officials had an eye out for him, and when the flag would go down, the Cowboy fans would chant: "15 yards, holding... Neely!" At one time they took up a collection in the stands to buy him another motorcycle.

He became hard-bitten and withdrawn, and for a while would submit to almost no interviews at all. His knees bear the scars of three operations, and his hand has been broken once. After the 1977 season he was scheduled for knee operation No. 4. He said, that's it, that's enough of football, and prepared to call it a career. The 1978 Super Bowl against the Denver Broncos, against Lyle Alzado, was to be his swan song after 13 years in the NFL.

The Cowboys' press book, which hunted for upbeat statements from the players, included a Neely quote couched in bitterness:

"What I'd like to do is come to camp and wear a baseball hat. It bugs me to be away from the family during training camp, but that's part of the game. What you have to do is lock that out of your mind."

Now he stood under the cloudy New Orleans sky, waiting for the first question. His face was a pro-football stereotype, hard-bitten, with a large lump of scar tissue on the bridge of his nose. It was cold, and Neely wore a blue and white wool cap—hiding hair that is graying rapidly—and a blue woolen warm-up jacket. The jacket, covering his pads and jersey, made him look enormous. The cap made him look much taller than his 6-6.

As he looked at his interrogator he closed his eyes slightly and tilted his head back, giving the impression that he was peering down the length of his nose ... literally looking down his nose. He seemed to be reaching down from a very great height. You almost felt like cringing. The answers were measured and nonexpansive.

He was not an easy interview; he was suspicious and wary, a striking contrast to the fun interviews Lyle Alzado usually conducts, interviews punctuated by bursts of raucous laughter—both from Alzado and the hordes of newsmen around him. Neely's interview was restrained but interesting:

Q. What was the attitude of your club going in to the 1970 Super Bowl, as compared to now?
A. You can't compare it because there's too many different people on the team. In 1970, in our Super Bowl, the first one against Baltimore, we were in there the first time. We didn't know what to expect. It might have been a distraction, I don't know. We should have won the game anyway but we didn't. Different people have different ideas about it.
Q. Have you always been a camera buff? (He carried a small box camera under his arm.)
A. No.
Q. Did you have a camera at your first Super Bowl?
A. Yes.
Q. Do you have an album at home of all the Super Bowl pictures?
A. I've just got boxes of pictures. Someday I'll do something with them.
Q. What have you taken today, just players standing around talking, doing things?
A. I'll take a picture of you guys.
Q. Why don't you sneak over to Denver and take a couple?
A. I don't think they'd like that.
Q. What can you tell me about Alzado? What about the last time he played against you last month?

What kind of a defensive end is he?

A. He's a very good defensive end. He plays the run exceptionally well. You might have a block on him, but to sustain a block is really difficult to do. He's exceptionally strong, and combine that with his quickness as a pass-rusher, he becomes the type of player who makes you stay mentally alert. If you have a mental lapse, if you try to outthink him or something, well—you can't do that. As long as I concentrate, I think I'll have a decent game with him.

Q. He says that, to him, the game is a street fight. He likes to keep the street fighter's image alive, yet when I watch him play I don't see him doing any crazy stuff or giving any cheap shots. Does he go a little bit nuts out there?

A. No, Lyle Alzado is a very classy ballplayer. He's not a cheap-shot artist.

Q. Did he ever spit at you? He said once he spat at you.

A. No, not that I know of. If he did he missed. Look, I don't play those games. When I'm playing football, I don't worry about the guy who talks, because when he's talking to me or trying to get me to do something, all he's doing is trying to cover up his own inadequacies.

Q. Besides, talking uses up breath.

A. At the level of conditioning that we are, that doesn't make any difference.

Q. Does Alzado remind you of anybody you've ever played?

A. No.

Q. Any of the NFC guys?

A. I don't fall for that trap. That's the one thing 13 years teaches you. You say he's as good as this guy, then the other guy gets mad; you say he's not as good, then he gets mad.

Q. Anyway, you don't have to worry about going against him next year.

A. No.
Q. Who are some of the better ones you have gone against?
A. I said I don't fall for that trap.
Q. Guys who are retired. Guys who were there when you broke in.
A. Well, I think probably one of the better ends I've known and always respected was Willie Davis of Green Bay, because he was a tremendous defensive end. And I don't know whether it was that he was in his heyday and I was just coming into the league or whatever, but I think Willie Davis—and probably also Bubba Smith—were the best. And my favorite was Jim Marshall. He was unbelievable.
Q. Did you ever play Doug Atkins?
A. Yeah, I played against Doug. It was toward the end of his career, down here when he was with the Saints.
Q. How tough an adjustment was it for you when you switched from right side to left side? Did it take a full year to do it?
A. No, it took about three or four years.
Q. What makes it so tough?
A. Well, it's the difference between being right-handed and left-handed. If you've been on the right side, you've been writing right-handed all your life and suddenly you have to start writing left-handed. It's the same deal.
Q. You played the right side in college all the time too?
A. Yes. I've always been a tackle, all my life.
Q. Did you play when you were a little kid? Little League?
A. No.
Q. Never played till high school?
A. It was ninth grade.
Q. How big were you then?
A. 5-6, 156 pounds.
Q. Were you bigger than all the other kids at that time?

A. No, I grew six inches and gained 40 pounds in one year.
Q. (From a fat interviewer). So did I, but I didn't grow any inches. (Neely just stares.) When was that, that you grew that much?
A. Between ninth and tenth grades in high school. I was so uncoordinated I couldn't walk and chew gum at the same time.
Q. Did you switch positions after the growth? Were you playing other positions?
A. No. I've always played tackle.
Q. Were you an emotional type of player when you were younger, when you were in high school or college?
A. Well, I don't know what you call an emotional-type player. You mean one who screams and yells all the time?
Q. No, one who gets rattled.
A. No.
Q. A player who flies off the handle or—you know what I mean.
A. No.
Q. You've always been low-key.
A. If a guy wants to push me I'll push back, but that's it.
Q. Did you play defense, too, in high school?
A. And college. I didn't come in with the substitution rule, unlimited substitution, until I was a senior in college. I was always the one who wasn't mean enough to play. That's what the coaches said.

Two writers sat in a rear seat on the official press bus. It was Wednesday, January 11, the first of two days of open interview sessions with all the players. One writer mentioned that he had talked to Ralph Neely the day before.

"I came away with frost on me," the guy said. "I'm doin' Alzado today—sort of a square-off press-

One Week to Kickoff

conference thing, the two guys who'll be battling each other on the line. What's Alzado like?"

"You'll have fun," the other guy said. "You won't come away with frost on you."

The dining room of the Sheraton, the Broncos' hotel, was decked out in press-conference decor. Each table carried the number of a player. You sat at the table of the player you wanted to interview. There were four chairs around each table, but at No. 77—Alzado's table—there were already eight or ten. The next table over, middle linebacker Randy Gradiashar's, had been stripped of chairs, a fact that was not lost on some of the Bronco players who streamed into the room.

Alzado wore a blue wool cap, Bronco tee-shirt, and jeans as he picked his way through the crowd to get to his table. There was no chair for him. Everyone stared. Finally one writer got up and joined the mob of radio men and reporters who had ringed the table, two deep. He didn't look happy. No one likes to lose valuable field position.

Alzado's table was the most heavily populated in the room. Craig Morton might have given him a battle, but the quarterback had been taken into a separate chamber. Reporters looking for an easy day's work naturally headed for Alzado; he ran them through the oft-repeated stories, added some new ones, and with endless patience, never seeming to be bored, treated all questions alike—the innocuous and the outrageous, the superficial and the probing—with politeness and wit and enthusiasm.

Q. What kind of family life did you have as a kid?
A. Well, my dad was never around, my mom worked and made $80 a week supporting six of us. There wasn't very much food around; didn't have very many clothes to wear. I don't want to sound like I'm the only one who's ever had it rough, because I'm not. But it was rough. I went to work, I picked

up garbage. People used to ask me in the summer, "Lyle, what do you do?" I used to tell them I was a garbiologist. They said, "You work in the science building?" I said, "Yup. Inwood Sanitation."

Q. How do you spell garbiologist?

A. Don't ask me, I worked in Inwood Sanitation.

Q. How many street fights would you estimate you've been in, Lyle?

A. I don't know. When I was going to grade school, junior high school, high school, it was almost every day.

Q. Did you ever get beat?

A. Me? You crazy? You know, there've been situations where I knew I had to be smart or be dumb, so I was smart and ran. Four and five and six guys, you don't hang around.

Q. What are some of the weapons you've used in street fights. How rough did it get?

A. Well, I used a—this sounds like I'm coming out of prison here—I carried a straight razor.

Q. Did you ever use it on anyone?

A. Yeah, a couple of times.

Q. How bad was the damage?

A. I didn't hang around to find out.

Q. Where are all of your boyhood friends now?

A. Well, I always know where six of them are, six that I was close to out of 20 or 25 guys I knew.... One particular guy—I don't want to mention any names—was a fullback on our high school football team, one of the meanest guys I ever met in my life. He got caught up in a dope-type thing and ended up in prison. The last time I saw him was about four years ago, and he had just gotten out; I don't know where he is now.

Q. If you held a class reunion, where would it be held?

A. I *had* a class reunion, just six or seven months ago, but I didn't go back. I asked my wife, "What do you think I should do? Do you think I should go back there?" And she said, "It depends on how you feel." I didn't want people to remember me the way I was. I wanted them to see what I'm doing now, and I didn't particularly want to go back there and talk about what we used to do—robbing gas stations, stealing candy, that kind of thing, you know?

Q. How often have you been jailed?

A. Let's just say a whole bunch.

Q. What was your longest stay?

A. Just an overnight thing. One time I stayed a night and a day and they let me out that following night. Minor things, you know. Once I was caught in a stolen car; and there were numerous street fights. I remember one time I got into a fight in a bar in Long Island called the Haven. A friend of mine threw the bouncer through a glass window and we took off. I didn't really do anything in the fight, for a change. Then the damned guys came to my apartment and knocked on the door. My mother answered the door and she turned to me and said, "Not again." And they towed me off to jail. Nassau County.

Q. How many times has your mother seen you play?

A. In person, only once. That was against the Chicago Bears in Denver in my second year. Terrible game. When I came off the field, do you know what she said to me? "I don't know how you can play that game. It's disgusting!"

Q. If your mom thought it was disgusting when you played ball, what did she say when you came home from the slammer?

A. My mom didn't know much about it because there were times when I didn't live at home. Sometimes I'd live with my buddy, Mark Lyons, so I'd be at his house.

Q. How many kids do you have, Lyle?

A. I don't have any yet. I've been married two years and six months. Probably next year I'll have little

Lyle. I'll make sure he doesn't live in the streets. I'll make sure of that.

Q. Does football seem not so dangerous compared to your old street days?

A. Hell, football is *easy* compared to that. You kidding me? I'm wearing a helmet and shoulder pads and a jock and all kinds of stuff to protect me. Out there you didn't protect yourself with anything.

Q. Ralph Neely can't carry a razor.

A. No, but he's a hell of a football player.

Q. When you were a teenager, did you and the guys you hung out with think pro football players were big stuff?

A. Nah, I didn't care. When I was a senior in high school, after my senior year, I thought football was really hot stuff. That's when I really got into football. And I'll never forget, the New York Giants had a luncheon and Scoop Gutterman, a guy who did something with the Giants—I don't know exactly what, maybe he did the laundry or something—said, "Lyle, you want to meet Frank Gifford?" I said, "Are you kidding me? Frank Gifford? Sure, I'll meet Frank Gifford." So I went over to Scoop Gutterman's house and sat there for about an hour or so looking out the windows, waiting for him to drive up. He drove up, walked over to me, and Scoop Gutterman said, "Lyle, this is Mr. Gifford." And Mr. Gifford said, "How are you, son? Nice to meet you." He put his arm around me and said, "Yeah, you're a big fellow, too." I was so impressed that he told me I was big.

Q. What's your initial reaction now, this circus, this forest of microphones...?

A. Tell you what, if I give you my home number and you call me the end of February, I'll let you know. Because right now I just don't know how to act because it's...the Broncos have never been in

anything like this before. They keep saying that
we're underdogs and the pressure will get to us.
You know, we'd be physical, we'd be no good.
They'll find out.
Q. What's the wildest thing that's happened to you,
along with Broncomania?
A. The parade. Fifty thousand people were out there. I
was sitting on the back, and they made us wear our
jerseys with our name on the back. People were
screaming and clapping and pounding on me and
they pulled me out of the back seat. I was sitting on
top of a Cadillac and they came in and pulled me
out of the car. I was lying on the ground. It
reminded me of Brooklyn.

On Thursday, January 12, the Broncos' wives and
girlfriends arrived on a special charter flight, along
with the club personnel. It was a high-spirited,
emotionally keyed-up group. They came storming into
the dingy Sheraton lobby, and they didn't notice the
depressingly heavy decor, or the worn cushions and
carpeting. They didn't get the message until later, when
they moved into their husbands' rooms and watched
the first cockroach scurry for cover.

Sharon Alzado had arrived earlier, by herself. "I
couldn't stand it in Denver anymore. I was so keyed up,
so tense I just had to be here," she said. A few people
who never met her before note that she's a pretty
woman—slim, with sandy-colored hair. She talks
quickly, the words pouring out on top of each other.
Her observations are fresh, often startling. She was a
breath of fresh air in the stultifying atmosphere of the
Sheraton.

On Thursday night a party of nine of us, including
Sharon's parents, Bill and Edith Pike, went to
Antoine's. The Oysters Rockefeller were spicy and
enticing, the shrimp remoulade pungent and biting, the
freshly made bouillabaisse terrific. The wine was a

1973 Louis Latour Meursault, a white Burgundy which was full-bodied and heady.

Antoine's was doing it up right for us. They were afraid not to. At the door our entrance had been blocked by a young maitre d' who took exception to the fact that Danny Davis, a Denver disc jockey and one of Alzado's closest friends, was not wearing a jacket and tie.

"Sorry, sir, but you must have a jacket at Antoine's."

Alzado whirled on the man, and his voice rattled the windows of that venerable establishment. "You go to hell!" he said. "You want to see this goddamn place torn apart?" But under his breath he had said to another captain: "This guy here is Craig Morton." One of the two approaches worked.

Later that night, near midnight, we were back at the Sheraton. Thirty or so Bronco people, in various shades of orange, were buzzing around the lobby. Lyle was sleeping. Sharon Alzado, still keyed up, sat in the dark, deserted restaurant and talked:

"These last few nights I just couldn't sleep; I did everything possible to get tired. Quarter to one last night I tried to fall asleep, but I lay there awake until 3:30. The last time I looked at the clock it was like 4, and I got up at 5 and washed my kitchen floor. I got an hour and a half of sleep last night and I'm not tired yet.

"Nothing like this has ever happened to me. I didn't believe we were going to the Super Bowl until Lyle left Monday, and it still didn't hit me till I landed here. But I couldn't sleep last night. I've been going on one and a half hour's sleep all day.

"When Lyle left, this whole thing seemed a little more real. The first week after the Oakland victory I didn't feel a thing. It only started to hit when they'd show the national spots on TV, when we'd hear 'The Dallas Cowboys and the Denver Broncos in the Super Bowl...' and it would be national coverage. I would say, 'That's *us*?' I probably won't really fully get the whole thing straight until the day before the game.

"I never felt it would be this way this season. My best friend and I had a little prediction pool at the beginning of the season, and everybody said 8-6. You know: new coach, tough schedule. And I don't know what possessed me, but I said 11-3. So I was up there. When we were 12-2 I didn't even hit the biggie, but I predicted 11-3.

"I always thought we were a playoff team, but I was thinking, possibly a wild card—because beating Oakland in our division seemed like a little too much to hope for.

"I don't know if I envisioned the Super Bowl. I've always wanted to come to New Orleans, and I thought this would be the only way I'd get there. Lyle would never put this on our list of places to visit. So in the back of my mind I was hoping for it, but I didn't think we'd get this far.

"But this Red Miller has been amazing. I love him. I mean the wives love him. And we *stay* with the players. Can you imagine that? What other coach would let the wives stay with the players before the Super Bowl?

"In Denver, the night before a game, they stay at a hotel. But that's just as well. If I had to get up the morning of a game and see how nervous he is . . . That's the worst thing. It won't be bad the evening before the game, but having to wake up with Lyle before the Super Bowl . . . I don't think I even want to talk to him.

"Lyle's preparation starts about Thursday for a game. He starts getting into his mood, but he definitely has mellowed a lot this year. Years before, when I first met him, you didn't talk to Lyle before a game. And you didn't talk to him if they lost, which they usually did in the early years of the Broncos. He was such an intense player, and he came from a winning high school team and a winning college team. He didn't cope with defeat very well.

"This year he's mellowed a lot, and he'll relax before the game. He used to go to the hotel about 7 at night—curfew is at 11, the night before the game—but this year he'd go at 9 or 9:30. So he was a lot more relaxed this year. But that wasn't until after he found out he could play after his injury. He was super-paranoid about coming back off of a knee injury in Cincinnati last year."

Saturday, January 14: Lyle Alzado and Danny Davis and a few of Lyle's Long Island friends—Mark Lyons, Ira Gordon, and Larry Schepps—are having breakfast at the Sheraton. Off to one side sits Dr. Jack Kahn, the private Florida chiropractor retained for Bronco middle guard Ruben Carter, and Alzado's in-laws, Bill and Edith Pike.

Sharon Alzado and Paula Davis enter the room. They are on their way downtown to catch a little more of New Orleans' pre-Super Bowl fever—its own special brand of Broncomania. Dr. Kahn eyes Sharon Alzado carefully, noting her jeans, her orange tee-shirt with the Lyle Alzado picture on it, and her orange boots.

"Pelvic displacement. A leading cause of pelvic displacement," the doctor says.

"What is?" someone asks him.

"Those boots she's wearing. A leading cause..."

Sharon and Paula Davis are not listening. They're busy telling everyone what they saw in New Orleans—the latest manifestations of a mania they know only too well.

"We were at Pat O'Brien's on Bourbon Street, and everybody was wearing orange. Every time somebody walked in with orange on, everybody in the place would stand up and cheer," Sharon said.

"There were a few people from Dallas, but they weren't loud: they just clapped when somebody played a Texas song. There were double pianos. One would play a Texas song, and then they'd play a Denver song, and they'd go back and forth."

One Week to Kickoff

Someone wanted an example of a Denver song.

"'*I wish I was in Colorado. If I had a wagon,*'" Paula sang, "'*If I had a covered wagon...*' Then we improvised. There's a song—I don't think you've heard it—the modern version of 'The Battle of New Orleans' with Denver Bronco words, and it's fantastic. 'Red Miller took his mighty team down the mighty Mississip'—and then there's a chorus, I wish I could sing it for you—'Take care of the Raiders and crush the iron curtain into tiny nuts and bolts...'

"'Crush the mighty Raiders,' no—its 'crush the iron curtain'—I don't remember the words. So we all sang that one, and then they played 'God Bless America' and everybody in the place stood up and put their hands over their hearts.

"There was a guy dressed totally in orange—orange tie, orange shirt, and one of those umbrella hats with Denver Broncos on and pins all over—he was unbelievable. He was just walking around for people to take pictures of him.

"By the time we left, the two pianists and a guy playing a tray all had on orange hats. They started out with all Texas songs—they were definitely for Texas—but when we left they were all wearing orange hats and were pro-Denver all the way. There was a guy from Pittsburgh who had on a Dallas hat, and as we left he grabbed me around the neck and said, 'You've converted me!' and stomped on it."

"Another song we have," Sharon said, "is Old MacDonald had a farm, only they changed it ...'Coach Red Miller had a team, E, I, E, I, O. And on his team he had Craig Morton, E, I, E, I, O. With a pass pass here, a pass pass there, here a pass there a pass everywhere a pass pass.' Then you go through all the verses and you say, 'Had a Haven Moses, with a catch catch here, a Jackson with an interception here, interception there, Alzado with a sack sack here, a sack sack there, Turner with a kick kick here, a kick kick there.' The whole place sang it. The whole place stood up and screamed that song.

"The people next to us were from Chicago and Detroit, and they were Denver fans. Others came from Oklahoma, Kansas City, Carolina. A friend of mine called from Minneapolis and said she was driving downtown and they had a great big orange sign that said GO BRONCOS hanging downtown.

"There was a group that grabbed us downtown at dinner—they said we're from Chicago and we're here rooting for you. They said you have to go downtown wearing orange, so that's why I put on my orange tee-shirt. They said if you don't have it on people look at you like you might be for Dallas. Everybody who sees anybody wearing orange—they run up and hug each other like they're long-lost friends.

"The Dallas people are very mellow. They just don't have the energy that Denver has. This is Denver's first year here, and it's like being back in high school. I'll never be the same again. People are driving down, coming any way they can; they're sleeping in driveways, and their energy level is incredible. The whole game is for Denver; all of Denver is involved in this game, and all of Colorado.

"When we left they had on the news a Denver couple who were leaving for New Orleans. They had rented a driveway here for $100 a night—to sleep in the car, in the driveway, in their own car, to be able to be here at the Super Bowl. People still don't have tickets. Twenty-five thousand people came from Denver and only 14,000 of them have tickets.

"You notice the interviews with the Broncos and the Cowboys themselves. Denver is loose; the players are being interviewed and someone's standing behind them making a face. They're knocking Denver for it, but that's how loose Denver is."

"I think everybody knows we're going to win, but even if we don't, the fans in Denver won't be aware that we lost. They love the Broncos," Paula Davis said. "Did you hear what Coors Brewery is doing this week? They're canning beer orange. *They're making it orange*. All over the city of Denver they're distributing orange beer.

"It's a high for the entire state, the entire region. Wyoming and everybody, they're all pulling like it was their own home team. You go into Denver today and there's nothing that you can buy that isn't available in orange. You can get an orange telephone for $29; you can have your car painted orange and they wash it off on Monday—you know, for the weekend. Of course you can buy orange shirts, orange shoes, orange bowling balls—at Christmas they even had orange Christmas trees. People decorated their houses orange for Christmas."

The girls got up and left. Bill Pike watched them leave, then reached into his pocket and brought out a card. He handed it to one of Lyle's Long Island friends.

"Thought this might interest you," he said. "It's a card Lyle and Sharon sent us last Christmas."

The card had a mouse on front, sitting on a Christmas ornament, with the words *Hi Hi Hi* over its head. Lyle's friend read it out loud.

"Dad: We also have Denver Broncos gym shorts for you, but we left them at home! So you can pick them up when you're in Denver next week. Love, Sharon."

"No, not that side. Read the other side," Bill Pike said.

"To Bill," he read. "I have never had a father before. I never thought I ever would. All the years that I needed to have a man around, there was none. Thank you. I finally have one—Father.

"Big Lyle #77."

SIXTEEN:

Super Bowl XII

THE BRONCOS have taken their warm-ups and are back in their dressing room in the bowels of the cavernous Superdome. It is hot. The field is warm, too. Muggy. Dead air. Bad for kicks.

Lyle Alzado is sweating slightly. He leans back toward the locker, tilts his head way back, closes his eyes. He is thinking about Ralph Neely. I'm gonna have the game of my life off this guy, he is thinking... the game of my life.

His locker is in an isolated area in the back, near the equipment room, off the main locker area. It's fine with him. He likes to be alone. When he first arrived at the stadium, Larry Elliott—the equipment man—told him, "You're back in the suite. You've got the penthouse." Fine. He liked to be alone.

Someone hollars: "Get yourselves ready! Five minutes! Defensive team will be introduced!" There isn't much noise from outside. Before the warm-ups the tape decks had been going, and a few guys had been dancing around—Riley Odoms, some others. Not now.

Red Miller's face appears in the doorway of Alzado's little room. He is smiling. He looks relaxed.

"You okay?"

Alzado nods.

Red Miller. The Redhead. Keep 'em loose, don't let 'em get tight. Will I ever be able to play for another coach? The Redhead. Stan Jones. I'm lucky, man. I've gotten coaches to play for.

The Redhead. Seventeen years an assistant coach in the NFL, putting in other people's offenses, watching them get the credit. God, how did he do it? It took the Dirty Dozen to bring him in here. And Fred Gehrke. I'll always be grateful to Fred for that. A bad scene. But something good came out of it.

Rap on Red was that he was a party guy. Reckless guy, liked the night life, ex-amateur boxer, didn't mind a drink or two. My kind of guy. Probably kept him from getting a head coaching job long before this. Rough-house Red. NFL owners don't go for that. Hasn't had a drink in a year and a half. Wouldn't even take a drink of champagne after we beat Oakland. What was it he said? "I quit drinking because I wanted to give myself every chance to become a head coach. If that was holding me back—and I'm not so sure it was—well, I didn't want to give them that excuse anymore."

A player's coach, boy. Get right down in the dirt with you. Got down in the pits with Claudie Minor. Pinned Kenny Brown. Went after the Steeler assistant coach, George Perles, under our stands. Played ragtime piano at the rookie show. What the hell did he say? "I'm a rookie, too." Hell of a man, Red.

No noise coming from the locker room now. What did Cliff Harris say when we played them last month? "I heard 'em singing 'Jingle Bells' in the locker room before the game—'Jingle Bells' with raunchy words: 'Dallas Cowboys, Dallas Cowboys, We'll whip their ass today.' Couldn't do that with Tom Landry around. Gol-lee, those guys aren't ready to play a football game." Well, screw him. I don't hear any 'Jingle Bells' today.

"OK, let's get out there!"

OK, all right, this is it.

The Cowboys offense is introduced first. Neely is the first player announced. He jogs through two lines of Cowgirls, and then stands at attention between the last pair. Leaning backward slightly, his back arched, he looks lean, rangy, self-assured.

Then come the Broncos. Chavous, Carter, Alzado,

Super Bowl XII

the front three. Alzado comes out too soon. "Hold it a minute," Dave Frei says. "Screw you, I'm going out! I can't wait!" Alzado says. Frei notices that he is crying. The Bronco player are pounding each other and slapping hands. Louie Wright leaps into the linemen's arms.

On the sidelines the Cowboys are slowly loosening up. A few of them watch the Broncos being introduced and turn away in disgust.

"We've got cheerleaders on the sidelines for that," Harris says.

"You show your emotions in the game, not the pregame," Harvey Martin says. "All that jumping around tires you out."

Jack Martilotta and Sal Ciampi are watching the game on TV at home. Ira Gordon, Mark Lyons, Dave Downey, and Larry Schepps are scattered through the stands.

"Watch Alzado's neck go up and down," Schepps says to the guy sitting next to him. "Watch his fingers. He's getting himself ready for battle."

Drew Pearson calls the toss for the Cowboys. He calls tails; and it comes up tails. Dallas receives. On the sidelines Alzado claps his hands once and reaches for a cup of ice water from a lage tray. His head is jerking up and down, his fingers twitch.

All the Bronco defensive players want the Cowboys to receive. They want first crack at Roger Staubach and the Cowboy offense in their own territory. Many newsmen also feel it would be a better play for Denver, having their defense on the field at the beginning against a cold Cowboy attack, rather than Craig Morton and the Broncos facing the Dallas defense. A couple of writers ask Miller if it was too far-fetched an idea—the idea of Denver winning the coin toss and kicking off instead of receiving.

"The defensive guys would love it," Miller says, "but I wouldn't count on it. Whenever we have to call a coin toss, all the offensive players on the sidelines are yelling, 'Win it! Win it!' and all the defensive guys are yelling, 'Lose it! Lose it!'"

With the Bronco defensive players it is a very serious thing, though. They had been talking about it all week in practice. They wanted first crack at the Cowboys. They had been reading all the Dallas quotes during the week, and their emotions were running high, even though they appeared loose and relaxed to outsiders.

"They're just like psychos," Alzado had said. "They can't wait for this game—absolutely cannot wait. When Dallas has the ball they're gonna get swarmed from so many differtent directions they won't believe it. We're gonna be swarming like flies.

"You ought to see what our practices have been like this week. Crisp. Efficient. I've never seen this kind of intensity. A few times it came very close to scrimmage conditions.

"Cliff Harris and Charlie Waters were saying what they're gonna do to us, Danny White was saying they're gonna have so much offense we won't know how to handle it. It all helps. And do you know what Henderson said? It's on our bulletin board back in Denver.

"He said, 'If Denver's in the Super Bowl, I'm gonna put a down payment on a house right now.' I love it. I love to hear stuff like that. Did you ever see Riley Odoms when he turns it loose on a block? He can be an awful mean dude, and he wants Henderson bad.

"Claudie Minor, now that's another mean guy. All he's thinking about, all he's talking about, is Too Tall Jones."

The Cowboys return the kick to their own 29. They try a reverse to their left side—Alzado's side—on their first play. Tom Landry is very big on opening the game with reverses. He opened Super Bowl X against the Steelers with a reverse to a linebacker on the kickoff, and the play made big yardage. Johnson fumbles the handoff on the reverse, though, and Tommy Jackson smothers the play for a nine-yard loss.

Testing me. The bastards are testing me right away with a damn reverse. Can you believe that crap?

They challenged me, and I'm glad of it. Let 'em run at me all day. If they do, we're gonna win this game. Neely blocked down on me from the outside. I saw the handoff all the way... grip Neely on top of the shoulders, steer him... watch the tight end blocking down... Okay, now hand-slide... let the tight end take his shot, then slide off it. I could spin, but Stan Jones doesn't want us spinning out this game. In the old days I'd have head-slapped the guy right off me. Head slap's illegal now. Damn! Anyway, I read the damn thing. I played it the way Stan wanted me to. Play the run first, then the pass.

Second and 19. Staubach hands the ball off to Tony Dorsett, again testing Alzado. He reads the play, pinches into the hole, avoids Neely's block entirely, and makes the tackle head-on.

Easy to read Neely on that one. Could tell the run was coming. When he sets to pass-block there's less pressure on his fingers, less discoloration. When he gets down lower to drive-block you can see the discoloration. This time he's down. I raise my right arm, like I'm set to ram him instead of pinch. Stan says they've picked up that key on me. So I give him the decoy and then pinch. Good shot on Tony D. Hurt him a little bit. Tough runner. Got to hit 'em tough to get 'em out of there.

Staubach completes an eight-yard screen right to Preston Pearson and the Cowboys punt. Alzado slides away from Neely, but Dorsett chops him at the knees. Morton hits Haven Moses for 21 yards, and the

Broncos need one first down to be in field-goal range. Alzado is standing on the side of the Bronco bench closest to the action. He claps his hands, shouts to the offense.

On third down Morton is thrown for an 11-yard loss by Randy White, the Cowboys' All-Pro right tackle. He comes in clean.

Damn! How'd he get in there that clean? Okay, forget it. Makes no difference at this stage.

The Broncos punt and miss their first big opportunity. Tony Hill, a rookie flanker, tries to field the ball on the 1-yard line, bobbles it, and just barely gets it back. The Broncos' John Schultz and Randy Rich are fighting him for the ball.

On first down, Staubach swings a pass to Dorsett over a blitzing Tommy Jackson on the left side for 15 yards—a gutsy call. Robert Newhouse, the fullback, cracks back on Alzado from the outside.

Watch those screens... they're holding the back in to chop back on me... the knee-breaker, the 'bastard block.' Should be illegal. I guess Red coached that block in New England, too.

On the next play Alzado slides inside and nails Dorsett for three yards.

Neely's looking intense, very intense. Not nervous, though. I'm beating him off the ball... stay underneath him... control him with my arms and strength. He can't match my strength: big guy, but not very strong. Quiet, though. Not a word out of him. Okay, I'll be quiet, too. Very unusual for me to be this quiet.

Dorsett is hit by Rueben Carter and Randy Gradishar on the next play, and he fumbles. Alzado is

Super Bowl XII

over the ball. John Fitzgerald, the Cowboy center, wrestles it away from him.

Sonofabitch! The guy ripped it out of my arms. Feel good about Neely, though. Can't block me. Gonna be a tight game, a defensive game—10-7, maybe, something like that.

Staubach is sacked by Carter and the Cowboys punt. The first quarter is half over and Dallas looks shaky. They haven't gotten out of their own territory. They had fumbled their first play, the reverse. They had messed up their first punt when they hit the Denver receiver before he got the ball, giving the Broncos instant field position. Then they messed up the Broncos' punt, fumbling it on their 1. And then Dorsett had fumbled. And still the Broncos hadn't gotten a point out of all this. A bad sign.

Morton tries a little dumpoff pass. Plop. Nothing on it. Randy Hughes intercepts. Broncos second defensive line goes in—Paul Smith, John Grant, and Brison Manor—and Cowboys punch it in for a touchdown; the scoring run, three yards by Dorsett, coming over Brison Manor, Alzado's replacement. Jones likes to use his second line on every third series. The party line is that there's no dropoff in talent, but no one believes it.

What the hell's he bringing them in for now, on our 25? Very disappointing. Can't understand that thinking. We had two short series. Nobody's tired. Why the hell couldn't they have put me in for that short yardage situation? I can stop one play, for Christ sakes.

Okay, seven points is all. Not bad. Not bad until it gets up there in double figures.

Next series Morton throws interception No. 2. Nothing on the ball. Good field position for Dallas.

We're in trouble. Craig's not right. Okay, here they come on offense. (Newhouse sweeps right for nine, Dorsett sweeps right for 18.) Running it away from me. Son of a bitch, they're running the other way! Think pursuit... chase everything... get off your butt and get down the line. Hurdle Neely on the sweep and the guard cuts me off. Risky... going for the knees... got to be around the ball, though. Might pick up a fumble.

First down, goal to go on Bronco 8. Dorsett tests Alzado on left side, met head on for no gain. Next down a passing down. Butch Johnson lines up next to Neely as a tight end. Doubles on Alzado. Quick pass. Incomplete. No chance to get to Staubach. Third and goal, Joe Rizzo blitzes, flushing Staubach to his left, where Alzado gets the sack.

Halo spinner. Drive seven yards upfield... here comes the blitz. Okay, hit a point seven yards deep and then drive back underneath. He's running. Gotcha, Roger! No talking to him. Not yet. Push off on him a little as I get up.

Neely still showing no emotion. Damn, I'm whipping the guy. A pro, though. No emotion. No talk.

Cowboys kick a field goal. Next Bronco series ends with Randy White pressuring Morton into a dumpoff pass for minus-eight.

Nervous time, now. Looks bad: defense playing like hell and we're still down, 10-0. Offense hasn't done a thing. We're in trouble... Got to get something on the board, anything. Damn, maybe defense can score a TD. Maybe I can. Wouldn't that be something, a touchdown in the Super Bowl? Maybe a Ron McDole play, tip the ball in the air and catch it in stride.

He's calling for the second defense. What the hell's going on? We weren't in two series, we were in one series? Got to talk to the man, at least stand next to him, at least talk to him after the season. Just Stan and me. Damn system's got to go.

Cowboy's drive on the second defensive line and kick a field goal. First defense comes back in when Cowboys reach Bronco 23. On third down Alzado flushes Staubach, who scrambles to his right. Alzado pursues and gets him right near the sideline. Just as he steps out of bounds, Staubach throws for an open Drew Pearson in the end zone and Billy Thompson intercepts. No interception. Staubach ruled out of bounds. Sack No. 2 for Alzado. Cowboys kick 42-yard field goal, and now it's 13-0 and Morton looks as if he could play 20 more quarters without cracking the Dallas defense for a touchdown.

Wondering when the hell Stan's gonna put me back in. Cursing, maybe he'll hear me, sonofabitch. Okay, first defense in, third and six. Play it in run-down defense, hit Neely. Oh, oh, a rollout! Outside fake, quick cut inside; hoping Staubach comes back inside, keeps going outside. Okay, buddy... 4.8 speed chasing you here. Can't really nail him, though—wrong angle. Slight hit out of bounds... where's the ref?... No flag, thank God.

"Hey, sorry there, Roger." Okay, don't way anything. "Fuck you."

First Bronco series and Morton throws interception No. 3, tying a Super Bowl record. Bronco defense has had a two-play rest, and now they're back on the field. Big defensive series for Alzado, though. His biggest of the game.

Newhouse tries his side on first down, but Alzado penetrates inside, forcing him to grab onto the jersey and drawing a holding penalty. Then two good pressures on Staubach: the first one when Neely tries a cut-block and Alzado hurdles him, the second when he drives Neely back into Staubach on sheer strength—forcing Staubach up and to his right, into the grasp of Carter. Net result of the series is minus-11 yards.

I'm in shock on that last interception by Craig. Something's really wrong here. We're going out there for our 30th play or something. We're gonna get beat if we don't stop this. Our offense is getting frustrated, you can tell by looking at their faces. Good play by Neely just then, hooking my jersey from in front: officials seldom see that, but this time they did. Officials been watching me close all game long, because of all this stuff in the papers about me punching and spitting and everything. Good! That means they'll be watching Neely, too. Arm drag to beat Neely on the next one... Roger sees me coming, gets out of the way. Hit him anyway after Ruben does. Hey, I'm dominating Neely. I'm having a day off him!

Broncos fumble the punt and Dallas recovers. Dallas misses the field goal against the second Bronco defense. Denver fumbles on its next series. Bronco turnovers now up to five. On third and long on Bronco 16, Staubach rolls right, gets pressure from Alzado, and dumps the ball off to Newhouse for one-yard gain. Field goal is missed. There will be two more Denver turnovers before the half—seven total.

Giving Neely help all the time now. Good-bye sacks, leaving the tight end in, sometimes a back. Only chance is on pursuit situation. Hey, halftime, time to regroup. Why the hell did they put our second defense in on two straight series at the end of the half? Nearly gave 'em a field goal! At least I got a hand on the field goal. Bernie Jackson came in on top and I got a hand on it...
I think we've seen the last of Craig. Can't stay in with the day he's having. Four interceptions! Hell, the guy's had a great year; today's just not his day.

Super Bowl XII

On Denver's first series of the third quarter, Jim Turner kicks a field goal, 47 yards, to get Denver on the board. Second longest field goal in Super Bowl history. Now it's 13-3.

Don't say a word to Jimmy before he goes in. Likes to be left alone, same as me. Hey, I'll be the first guy to shake his hand. What the hell, he got us three. We're not exactly tight, Jimmy and me, but today he got us three...

Cowboys first series of the second half ends with Staubach scrambling on third-and-long, picking up three yards. Tackle by Gradishar, flushes by Alzado.

Hook underneath, get upfield, use my inside arm to slap Neely away, come back underneath. So long Ralph, you're not blocking me today. He hasn't adjusted; he's not doing a thing different in the second half—and getting beat just as bad.

Broncos offense still with Morton quarterbacking, runs three plays and out. First defensive line played only one series, three plays, but now the Bronco seconds are in. Cowboys drive for a TD on Butch Johnson's leaping catch on a deep-post pattern. Dallas 20, Denver 3. Broncos' second defense has allowed 17 of the 20 points.

No pressure on Staubach on that post, no pressure. It's good-bye ballgame, folks. No way to do anything now. Hey, this is the game I wanted to score a touchdown in! No way to do anything; he's rotating the lines too much. Now it's on pride, on guts... Ah, hell!

Norris Weese replaces Morton at quarterback and the Broncos put seven on the board, but time is running out. The game is slipping away. On the third from last play of the third quarter, Neely drives low on a cut-block, and Herbert Scott, the left guard, piles on. Alzado's hamstring pops.

The second Bronco defensive line comes on the field, and Staubach tries a screen pass to Dorsett on the right side. Billy Thompson knifes through to spill him for a four-yard loss on a low, driving tackle.

Dorsett limps out on a twisted right knee. He is through for the day, but a few yards away, John Grant—the Broncos' backup middle guard—is writhing in agony and gripping his right knee. Scott, a third-year pro out of Virginia Union, had peeled back and hurled his 250 pounds at the back of Grant's leg a flagrant clip that was not called by the officials.

Two plays later Staubach would leave the game with a damaged right hand, and Cliff Harris would knock both himself and Rick Upchurch out on a violent collision on a pass route over the middle. Louie Wright, Denver's All-Pro left cornerback, had already been removed when his right shoulder popped out. It was popped back into place, and he came back into the game. Randy Gradishar, the Broncos' All-Pro middle linebacker, had been taken out when he sprained a previously damaged right ankle. They taped him and sent him back in. The Cowboys' left cornerback, Benny Barnes, was through for the day with a sprained right foot.

As Grant lies on the field moaning, and the Apache Belles from Tyler, Texas, go through their number on the sidelines, the PA system announces: "The turnstile count is 76,400; we thank you for attending the Super Bowl in New Orleans."

It is Rollerball, NFL style, and Alzado stands on the sidelines, watching Grant and rubbing his own hamstring.

Alzado comes in for one more series. Danny White is the Cowboys' quarterback. Alzado shakes his leg between plays, trying to get loose. On third-and-nine he beats Neely to the outside; Danny White sees him

Super Bowl XII

coming and dumps the ball off; Alzado takes a bead and drills White, low and hard—and late. The referee, Jim Tunney, watches the play from its inception; he watches carefully, crouching over White like a lifeguard trying to breathe life back into a drowned swimmer, finally signaling no penalty.

On the sidelines Jones watches Alzado getting up slowly, then signals for Brison Manor to replace him.

"I thought it was his knee," Sharon Alzado says to her father in the stands. "I was scared to death. Then I saw them taping his leg on the outside of his pants. I've never seen that before."

Alzado has had it for the day. He sits on the bench and watches the Cowboys score once more to win Super Bowl XII, 27-10. When the final whistle sounds, Ralph Neely comes over and seeks him out on the bench. They say something, shake hands, and leave the field.

Epilogue I

THE DOOR to the Broncos' postgame party room opened, and half a dozen Dixieland musicians walked in, followed by a crush of fans—some with invites, most of them without.

Two Bronco offensive linemen put their hands to their ears to try to shut out the deafening music pounding at their already aching heads. In the driveway outside the Sheraton, John Grant, his knee torn up by a clip, stumbled and fell to all fours in the darkness. A fan helped him up.

"I'm all right," Grant said, leaning heavily on the man. "I'll be all right."

Pete Rozelle and his wife, Carrie, were talking to Craig Morton at a table in the corner.

"You had two shots," the commissioner was saying. "The fumble on the one-yard line that they got, and the one where Riley Odoms was wide-open and Too Tall hit your arm."

"Yeah, I know," Morton said, staring at the floor.

"Think of it as a whole year," Rozelle said. "One great year." Morton nodded and thanked him.

The Bronco defense had not been embarrassed. "You know, you stop 'em, then we turn the ball over, then you stop 'em again and we turn the ball over again," Lyle Alzado was saying. "Do that seven times in one half, and your chances ain't too hot."

The stat sheet credited him with six unassisted tackles, an assist, and two sacks. Dallas' Harvey Martin won half a Super Bowl car on two tackles, no assists, and two sacks.

"Seems wrong, doesn't it?" Alzado said. "Okay,

Randy White—I could see him—but *Martin*? A guy gets the quarterback, and that wins him a car? I guess it's too much to ask—a guy on a losing team—thinking of anything like that. But Harvey Martin? Christ!"

He stood off to one side, trying to find a spot on the periphery of the crowd, but it was impossible. They were everywhere—orange hats, orange shirts, crowding by with plates from the buffet piled high with food.

"I can't eat anything," Alzado had told his wife earlier. "I'm feeling a little sick right now. Nauseous. I've got to come down from this game. It's taking a long time."

"You want to go upstairs?" Sharon said.

"What the hell, I'll stay down here. You don't go off and hide when you lose a ballgame. Let the fans have their party."

A tall, angular young man stopped by and shook Alzado's hand. He was Mark Mullaney, the Vikings' reserve defensive end and a Denver resident.

"Hey, you had a hell of a game," Mullaney said. "Where do you go now?"

"Pro Bowl," Alzado said.

"On that leg?" Mullaney said, remembering the pop of Lyle's hamstring.

"Yeah, I'll play," Alzado replied. "I wanna play in the damn thing. First one for me. Hey, is Marshall gonna retire?"

"Never," Mullaney said.

"Artie Shell almost retired him last year," someone offered.

"Yeah," Mullaney said, "and this year, when we played Oakland, all of a sudden I was the starting right end. They killed us, man."

A girl came by and wanted Alzado to sign her hat. He signed it. Then two ticket stubs. Then a TV man called him over for an interview. And a radio man. Then he signed a fan's jacket. And another ticket stub.

"C'mon," he said to a few friends. "Let's go next

door and sit down for a few minutes. I gotta get myself together."

In the locker room after the game, a wire service reporter told him Neely had paid him a tribute. The guy said Neely told him he'd won a few battles and lost some, and Alzado had played a good game—a sentiment first expressed in person, when he had sought out Alzado on the Bronco bench after the final whistle.

The quote wasn't entirely accurate. Neely, who had ended a 13-year career the day before, had said of Lyle on Dallas radio: "I won some battles and lost some, but evidently I won more than I lost. Some of those battles I lost were when he was doing what I wanted him to. Misdirection, play-action stuff. You have to go with misdirection against him."

"Yeah, misdirection," Alzado said. "Ask him how come they started running everything to the other side."

"I honestly think I had one of the best games of the year," Alzado said in the quiet of the dining room off the main party room. "My wife always tells me how I played. If I have a bad one she tells me. Today she... ah, what's the difference?

"Neely couldn't block me at all today. Sure, I made a couple of mistakes, but who doesn't? I got my pass-rush going, so they started doubling and tripling me. They were running the other side, and I was making tackles in pursuit. I thought I should have stayed in the game more. That's really what I thought."

The Cowboys had scored 24 of their 27 points against that second group.

Before the score became 27-10, the Broncos' first defensive line had played 38 plays. Dallas had gained 112 yards on them, but against the Broncos' second unit Dallas had gained 192 on 26 plays. Dallas had tried running the ball seven times to Alzado's five while he was in. Net gain: eight yards.

"They rotated me too much," Alzado said. "I think I could have made more things happen. I'm gonna talk to Stan Jones about it. I've gotta talk to him. I can't be taken out of the game like that, especially when I'm having the day I was having.

"He's gotta let me play more. The system is good—it works—but sometimes when you stay out too long you get cold. That's how I popped the hamstring.

"They should have changed quarterbacks at the half. That's what they should have done. Craig's done a super job for us this year, but you know, when a guy doesn't have it ...

"Neely really said that, that he won more battles? Lemme tell you, the guy couldn't block me. I was outmaneuvering him. On the run I was powering him, and on the rush I was quicker than he was. I knew I could do it all week. I just wish they'd have left me in the game more. I could have created a lot more things. But it just didn't happen.

"They kept putting me in and out. I had to regroup myself. I've got to play more."

On his last play, Alzado had said something to White.

"Yeah, I remember that," Alzado said.

"I told him, 'I wish I could have gotten you more.'"

"Did you know that Shirley Horner was down here this week?" Sharon Alzado asked a friend. "Lyle's old girlfriend from Yankton. She came down here to see Lyle and talk to him."

"Did you see her?" someone asked Sharon.

"I saw her," Sharon said. "You know, I always figured she'd be better-looking."

Epilogue II

Monday morning, January 16: We are sitting around Lyle Alzado's room at the Sheraton, watching his wife pack his gear for the Pro Bowl. He lies on the bed, occasionally grunting when he shifts the leg with the stretched hamstring muscle. His brother, Billy, sits by the window.

"What the hell do you need the Pro Bowl for?" Billy Alzado says.

"I need it because I want to play in it; because it's a thrill to play in a game like that."

The Cowboys' 27-10 victory is a bigger memory. So is the MVP award—shared by Randy White, the Cowboys' defensive right tackle, and Harvey Martin, their defensive right end.

"Two sacks and two tackles and he's the MVP," Alzado had said. "How can Harvey look at himself in the mirror this morning?"

There had been bitter postgame moments. The usual crowd of reporters had questioned Alzado, and a radio man had asked him: "How come you guys couldn't keep the pressure on Staubach?"—he'd been sacked five times—and Alzado kept telling them, "How the hell can you win with 11 turnovers?" Increasing the damage by three. He was the last one out of the locker room, as usual, and the team bus had been kept waiting. Jim Turner told someone, "We'll go as soon as the presidential press conference is over," tossing a look in Alzado's direction.

Now, on Monday morning, Billy and Lyle Alzado sit staring out the window and all of a sudden Billy's face brightens: "Hey, Lyle, you ever tell them about the time they threw me out of that ice cream joint, and I came and got you?"

"Yeah," Lyle Alzado says. "I was sleeping, and you woke me up and said, 'Lyle, there's work to do...'"

"Remember the way all those guys came out of the woodwork, Lyle? Like ants. Just like ants..."